The publisher of this book is generously donating all royalties from the retail sales of **"WORRY-FREE DIVORCE"** to:

LEMONADE DAY

America was built on the back of small business. Entrepreneurs take risks believing they can realize their dream if they work hard, take responsibility and act as good stewards of their resources. Today's youth share that optimism, but lack the life skills, mentorship and real-world experience necessary to be successful. In 2007, founder Michael Holthouse had a vision to empower today's youth to become tomorrow's entrepreneurs through helping them start, own and operate their very own business… a lemonade stand.

Lemonade Day is a strategic 14-step process that walks youth from a dream to a business plan, while teaching them the same principles required to start any big company. Inspiring kids to work hard and make a profit, they are also taught to spend some, save some and share some by giving back to their community. Since its launch in 2007 in Houston Texas, Lemonade Day has grown from serving 2,700 kids in one city to 1 million children across North America. With the help of partners like Google for Entrepreneurs, Lemonade Day will continue to spark the spirit of entrepreneurship and empower youth to set goals, work hard, and achieve their dreams.

You can learn more about Lemonade Day by visiting:
www.LemonadeDay.org

WORRY-FREE DIVORCE

Leading Divorce Professionals Speak

By Remarkable Press™

Worry-Free Divorce/ Mark Imperial. —1st ed.

Managing Editor/ Stewart Andrew Alexander

ISBN-978-0-9987085-9-1

CONTENTS

A NOTE TO THE READER

Thank you for buying your copy of "Worry-Free Divorce: Leading Divorce Professionals Speak." This book was originally created as a series of live interviews, that's why it reads like a series of conversations, rather than a traditional book that talks at you.

I wanted you to feel as though the participants and I are talking with you, much like a close friend, or relative, and felt that creating the material this way would make it easier for you to grasp the topics and put them to use quickly, rather than wading through hundreds of pages.

So grab a pen, take notes and get ready to learn some fascinating insights and real world experiences.

Warmest regards,

Mark Imperial
Author and Radio Personality

INTRODUCTION

"Worry-Free Divorce: Leading Divorce Professionals Speak" is a collaborative book series featuring leading Divorce Professionals from across the country who are passionate about helping people facing divorce.

Remarkable Press™ would like to extend a heartfelt thank you to all participants who took the time to submit their chapter and offer their support in becoming 'Get the word out Ambassadors' for this project.

Remarkable Press™ has pledged 100% of the royalties from the retail sales of this book to be donated to Lemonade Day.

Should you want to make a direct donation, visit their website at: www.LemonadeDay.org

JASON L. HURST, ESQ.

Attorney/Partner
Harrison & Held, LLP

Email: jlhurst@harrisonheld.com

Website: http://harrisonheld.com/professionals/jason-l-hurst

LinkedIn: https://www.linkedin.com/in/jasonhurstlaw

Facebook: https://www.facebook.com/JasonLHurstLaw

Avvo Attorney Profile: Jason Lee Marcus Hurst

Call: (312)-621-5253

Mr. Hurst has practiced exclusively in the area of Family Law since 2010, handling matters related to divorce, custody, child support, parenting time disputes and the preparation of premarital agreements. Mr. Hurst joined Harrison & Held, LLP in 2015 after having spent 5 years practicing at one of Chicago's premier Family Law firms. There he practiced in both the Family Law and Sports and Entertainment Family Law divisions of the Firm, where the firm's representation was focused on representing high-profile and high-wealth individuals.

During the course of his career Mr. Hurst has represented many current and former professional athletes, members of the media and a Grammy award winning Chicago musician, amongst the countless other hard working teachers, police officers, entrepreneurs and other professionals that he has had the pleasure of working with.

Mr. Hurst brings his wealth of knowledge and experience in the area of Family Law to Harrison & Held, where he continues to focus his practice on complex Family Law matters with the highest level of diligence, attention to detail and professionalism, treating every client as if they were his only client.

CHAPTER 13 DIVORCE
By: Jason L. Hurst

Describe the clients you work with and the types of situations they find themselves in when they come to you for your help?

I am a Family law attorney licensed to practice law in the State of Illinois. The umbrella of Family Law encompasses matters including divorce, child support, visitation disputes (now known as parenting time in Illinois), custody disputes (now known as allocation of parental responsibility in Illinois) and the preparation of premarital and post-nuptial agreements. During the course of my career I have represented many current and former professional athletes, members of the media and a Grammy Award winning Chicago musician, among countless other hardworking teachers, police officers, entrepreneurs and other professionals that I have called clients.

The majority of my practice is devoted to divorce work. As a part of handling someone's divorce, in addition to dividing marital assets and liabilities, I often must address some of the other Family Law issues mentioned above i.e., child support, allocation of parenting time and allocation of parental responsibility as most of the divorcing couples that I deal with have children.

For me, divorce issues fall into one of two major categories. The first, and I believe most important issue in a divorce case is child-related issues. Specifically, these issues pertain to parental responsibility, or which parent or parents will make major decisions affecting the child. In Illinois these decisions are broken into four categories: educational decisions e.g., whether your child goes to a public or private school and what specific school the child will attend; medical decisions e.g., who will be the child's pediatrician; religious decisions e.g., whether the child will be raised Catholic or Protestant; and extra-curricular activities e.g., whether the child will participate in swimming, soccer, both or neither.

The second major category of issues that must be addressed in a divorce proceeding is financial issues. This encompasses the division of assets e.g., who gets to keep the marital home and how retirement assets are divided; the division of liabilities e.g., who will have to pay the balance on those credit cards that were used to take family vacations; the payment of child support; and the payment of alimony (in Illinois maintenance or spousal support).

The individuals that come into my office are contemplating or have decided to dissolve their marriage; are unmarried and have a child in common with someone for whom they are seeking child support, parental rights, parenting time or contribution to child-related expenses; and unmarried persons who will soon be getting married and are looking to protect assets, income and/or shield themselves against their soon-to-be spouse's debts/liabilities by way of a premarital agreement. I help them to navigate the malaise of dealing with Family Law issues and to achieve their desired objectives.

What common obstacles prevent the working professionals you help from achieving their goals during a divorce proceeding?

A client may face many obstacles during the course of a divorce proceeding – some real and some perceived. The first obstacle to achieving any desired outcome is to arrive at and set clear goals. When I am meeting with a client for the first time, I learn the backstory i.e., what brought them into my office. Next, I learn the objective. The objective usually morphs during the course of our initial discussion as I explain the law to him or her, what their rights are, and possible/likely outcomes based on the facts of their case. It is during this process that we crystalize the goal(s). These goals may include receiving more of the liquid assets of the marital estate, preserving retirement assets, receiving more illiquid assets such as real estate, maximizing time with children, preserving an interest in a business without dividing the business interest with a spouse, maximizing a spousal support award and the list goes on depending on the unique facts and circumstances of the client's life. One thing however is clear; travelling down this road without clearly defined goals in an obstacle itself, and one which creates many pitfalls along the way.

A corollary to the obstacle of not having clearly defined goals is the obstacle of having the wrong goals. To understand the appropriateness of your goals, you must understand the why. For example do you want to keep the marital residence because you have spent many years perfecting your man cave, garden, den, et cetera, notwithstanding the fact that it would likely be more beneficial to your children that your spouse remain there with the children? Do you want more parenting time with your children simply because you hope to pay less child support? Do you object to your spouse moving out of state with the children simply as a means of asserting control over your soon-to-be ex-spouse? Do you object to your spouse having more time with the children because it may reduce your child support award? Are you foregoing your job search at the moment because landing a well-paying job will thwart your efforts at receiving maintenance? There are a myriad of ways that the divorce process can be used and/or manipulated to hurt the other party and/or pursue selfish interest – especially when children are involved. Having the wrong objectives almost invariably causes more litigation which cost you more money. No matter how clever you think you may be in pursuing your self-interest, the underlying motivations are usually transparent. This causes the other side to dig in and vigorously fight against these wrong-headed objectives.

The final obstacle is a corollary of the first two, which is having unreasonable goals or expectations. I am often asked by clients, "So when am I going to be divorced?" To which I must respond, well Mrs. Doe, your case was filed last Tuesday, so it will probably take a little longer. Or, I am asked, "So why do I have to pay my wife spousal support?" To which I respond, because Mr. Doe, you were married to Mrs. Doe for twenty-five years during which time she stayed home and raised all four of your children.

Having unrealistic expectations will lead to poor case strategy in pursuit of your unrealistic goals, which will cost you time and money. This obstacle is as much the lawyer's problem as it is the client's problem. Here, it is incumbent upon the lawyer to set realistic expectations at the beginning of the case and manage expectations throughout the case. If your lawyer ever promises you that you will obtain everything that you are seeking – run. You have either set the bar really low, your lawyer is terribly misinformed about the facts and/or law in your case or worse – your lawyer is lying to you. For most good attorneys, the answer to nine out of 10 questions is maybe or, it depends. Set clear goals. Set the right goals. Set realistic goals!

How do you help working professionals to overcome the obstacles often associated with divorce or Family Law matters?

Chapter 13 of Title 11 of the United States Bankruptcy Code allows individual debtors to propose a plan to reorganize their financial affairs to pay their creditors. Divorce is a full-scale reorganization of your life. Divorce may change where you live, the trajectory of your retirement, when you spend time with your children, how you shop and a myriad of other facets of life as you knew it. I try to help individuals reorganize their lives incidental to divorce proceedings in the most efficient and least disruptive manner possible under the circumstances. As in the case of a bankruptcy, you must have a plan to navigate the divorce process if you want to seamlessly transition to the next chapter of your life.

Above we discussed three obstacles to achieving your desired results in your divorce or other Family Law matter: failure to set clear goals; setting the wrong goals; and setting unrealistic goals. As a part of the initial meeting where goals are discussed and set, we also discuss a plan for achieving these goals. We determine what motions may need to be filed in the immediate future to achieve short-term goals; we discuss what facts and evidence must be gathered to achieve long term goals; and we discuss the range of possible outcomes based on the information that we have available at the time.

Shortly after the case is filed, we initiate the discovery process, which is the process of gathering evidence, documents, facts and information relating to the marital estate, the other party, potential witnesses and the case in general. As the discovery process unfolds, objectives and goals may morph over time as new information becomes available. It is important to re-evaluate and reassess the case frequently. I am therefore in constant contact with the client, discussing new information as it comes in and adjusting case strategy as goals are adjusted due to the new information that we receive.

Litigation requires that both the attorney and the client be nimble, flexible and adaptable. Moreover, it requires an intense level of focus on the objective/goals even as they are constantly evolving in a dynamic and changing case. This is how I help my clients to achieve their desired results in a divorce or other Family Law matter – I communicate with the client, collaborate with the client, crystallize goals and pursue them with a singular focus.

When it comes to the divorce process, what common myths or misconceptions do your clients believe to be true?

There are many myths or misconceptions surrounding the divorce process. One of the more frequent questions asked by potential clients is whether he/she should file for divorce first. Procedurally, there is no inherent advantage to filing for divorce before your spouse. The court does not view the other party less favorably because you filed first, assuming that there must be some serious character flaws to the other party. Likewise, the court does not view you less favorably for filing first and "abandoning" your family. This touches upon another common misconception - fault, which we will address below. However, once you do file for divorce, you have all the remedies of the divorce laws in your state available to you.

If your spouse has cut you off financially, this may create impetus for you to file first so that you can petition the court for things like temporary child support and temporary maintenance. If your spouse is busy squandering your savings on a gambling binge, you can and should file first to avail yourself of the Court's injunctive remedies to stop the outflow of cash. In this regard, there may be circumstances unique to your situation which makes it advantageous for you to file first; however, you do not win points on some theoretical scorecard for beating your spouse to the courthouse.

Another common misconception relates to the nature and extent of fee-shifting provisions. I do not work - therefore my spouse must pay all of the attorneys' fees for our divorce, right? In Illinois, attorneys' fees are first and foremost the responsibility of the party that incurred them. However, there are fee-shifting provisions in the Illinois Marriage and Dissolution of Marriage Act that allow a party to seek fees from his or her spouse during the pendency of the divorce proceeding. These fee payments however are not exactly what they seem to be.

In Illinois, a fee award during the pendency of the case (an interim fee award) is treated by the court as an advance against the receiving party's share of the marital estate. The party receiving the fee award should be credited with this payment when deciding the ultimate allocation of the marital estate. If you think of the marital estate as a balance sheet containing assets and liabilities, the fee award paid to the receiving spouse should count on his/her side of the ledger when adding up the assets awarded to each spouse. While the recipient spouse has forced his/her spouse to "pay" his/her fees by way of the fee petition, what they have really accomplished is moving money from one part of the marital estate to another part of the marital estate.

There are other fee-shifting provisions under Illinois law whereby a divorcing spouse can request that the other spouse contribute to his/her fees so that it does not count against the requesting/receiving party's ultimate share of the estate; however, the example cited above is the most frequently used mechanism for requesting fees from the other party.

The last and perhaps most egregious misconception in my opinion, is the concept of winning and losing in divorce court. I have been asked by potential clients, "how many of your cases have you won?" My answer is always the same – I do not believe that anyone wins in divorce, least of all children. Social science has taught us that children are generally better off when they grow up in healthy two-parent households.

Divorce breaks up families, depletes marital estates and usually forces everyone involved to reduce their standard of living to some degree. People who ask this question are usually looking to use the process as a tool "win" some form of retribution against their soon-to-be ex-spouse that has wronged them. This is foolhardy, an abuse of the system and process and a waste of both parties' time and money.

What unknown pitfalls should working professionals be aware of when seeking legal guidance?

I would not hire a dermatologist to exam a swollen ankle any more than I would hire a podiatrist to look at a rash. Both are doctors, but they each have different and unique experiences, training and skill sets. When seeking representation for your divorce you must avoid the pitfall of hiring a lawyer instead of hiring a Family Law lawyer.

Family Law is its own unique substantive area of law. It has nuances and some concepts which are not exactly intuitive. It is therefore important that you find a lawyer well-versed in this substance and nuance – someone that routinely practices in the area of Family Law. I have observed general practitioners and lawyers that practice in other areas of law try to muddle their way through a divorce proceeding – it is painful to watch. It is even more painful, frustrating and exasperating when I have the misfortune of having one of these ambitious lawyers as opposing counsel. It is counterintuitive, but I often tell my clients that it is much easier having a good lawyer as opposing counsel than a bad one. The good lawyer will know matrimonial law, know the rules and procedure and have a good handle on how the case can and should be settled.

In addition to finding an experienced Family Law practitioner, it is also prudent to find someone that practices in the specific locale in which your case is going to be filed. The State of Illinois is broken into twenty-four judicial circuits, the largest of which is the Circuit Court of Cook County.

The substantive divorce laws in Illinois are promulgated by the legislature and obviously apply to the entire state. However, each of the twenty-four judicial circuits passes its own set of local rules governing the process and procedure by which Family Law cases are handled in that judicial circuit.

These rules affect the discovery process, the form and substance of certain pleadings, alternative dispute resolution mechanisms and how Family Law cases are managed by the court from start to finish.

My practice is concentrated in Chicago (Cook County) and the surrounding suburban counties, which include Kane County, DuPage County, Lake County, McHenry County and Will County. I therefore make it a point to know the local rules in all of the counties in which I practice. When trying to avoid the incompetency pitfall, do not just hire a lawyer that is competent at practicing Family Law, hire someone that is competent at practicing Family Law where you live.

I can tell you from personal experience that handling a divorce case in Cook County is slightly different than handling a divorce case in DuPage County, which is slightly different than handling a divorce case in Will County. You do not want your lawyer to find out about the nuances of divorce practice in different areas or regions of your state in the middle of your case. Do your homework!

What are your clients most common fears surrounding the divorce process?

The inherent uncertainty of the divorce process makes clients very nervous. How much is my divorce going to cost? How long will my divorce take? How am I going to support myself and/or my children after the case is over? These are some of the common fears and concerns that new clients have. I never make the mistake of predicting the cost of a divorce or the time that it will take to divorce a client. I have had divorce cases take three months and I have had cases take three years, or longer. In short, the clients are wondering how they are going to survive the process and whether they will be left emotionally battered and financially ruined at the end.

The cost of your divorce and the time commitment are inextricably intertwined. Generally, the longer your case drags on, the more it will cost. The recurring theme of this chapter is to come in with a clear understanding of the process (it is your lawyer's job to explain the process to you and what to expect) and a clear understanding of what your objectives are. In that regard, I think that it is important to take an inventory at the beginning of the case of what you and your spouse agree on.

For example, do you both agree that the children will primarily reside with mom, and that mom should keep the marital residence to provide stability and continuity for the children, or vice versa? Do you and your spouse agree that you two should jointly make decisions affecting the health, education and welfare of your children? Taking inventory at the beginning helps to distill what the issues or contested matters in the case will be. This will save both parties time and money as resources are not otherwise being wasted where they don't have to be.

Aside from the cost and time commitment that divorce may require, there is the ever-looming fear relating to financial health and security, or lack thereof. Accordingly, divorce requires a certain level of financial planning. When parties separate, they are leaving a situation where husband and wife shared one set of expenses; after divorce, the parties are living separately, each with their own mortgage or rent payment, utility bills, food and transportation costs.

This may be especially daunting if you functioned as a stay-at-home parent or homemaker during the marriage and your spouse was solely responsible for supporting the family financially. I therefore counsel clients on how to structure their divorce agreements in a manner that provides them with the liquidity and cash-flow needed to meet their expenses after divorce.

This discussion usually also involves a candid dialogue about reducing expenses because the client is no longer sharing in certain expenses with their now ex-spouse. I try to help clients overcome all of these fears i.e., the time commitment of a divorce, the costs, their concern over their financial health, and many others, by tackling them head-on. I do so by working with clients at the beginning of their case to distill their objectives and then articulating a plan to help them achieve their desired results.

It sounds obvious, but why would your clients want to have a smooth and seamless transition to the next chapter of their lives?

At our core, we all want to provide secure, stable, comfortable lives for ourselves and for our children. If this is the underlying objective, you must approach the divorce process with the aim of making the transition from one chapter of your life to the next as smooth as possible. Remember the Chapter 13 theme – divorce is the wholesale reorganization of your life. You must approach the process psychologically with an eye toward planning for the future, not dwelling on past wrongs, transgressions, disappointments, heartbreak, letdown and failures. Distraction leads to litigation – litigation cost money.

You want to achieve the reorganization process incurring as little transactional costs as possible. Here, the transactional cost is attorneys' fees. It is easy to get distracted during the process. I once represented a nice woman who began the divorce process with the best intentions of getting divorced quickly and amicably. This goal however was soon derailed after she learned for the very first time during the case that her husband purchased a condominium in another city during the marriage without her knowledge or consent.

The city happened to be one that the husband frequently traveled to for work. The purpose of the condo was, as you may have already guessed, to entertain women while he was away on business. The case quickly took a nasty turn where unreasonable settlement positions were staked and deeply rooted in principle and the conviction that retribution was due.

When you are distracted by your spouse's infidelity or other transgressions, your objectives get distorted and your decision-making is not optimal. Distraction causes your focus to shift from securing your and/or your children's financial future to exacting retribution on your soon-to-be ex-spouse. To be clear, dishonesty, betrayal, abandonment and other symptoms of divorce are hurtful and have a very real emotional impact on the parties which may in turn impact the litigation. My point is simple; do not let emotion usurp your most basic human need and desire – survival. Survival is why you want to achieve the efficient, amicable reorganization of your life.

What led you to this field?

When I was 11 years old, I watched my parents go through a fairly acrimonious divorce. I can clearly discern how divorce changed my life and how my childhood looked and felt a little different after the divorce than before the divorce. I have seen and felt the impact of divorce firsthand. I had occasion to meet the lawyer that represented my mother a couple of times during the divorce, under what circumstances I cannot recall as this was some twenty-five years ago.

However, what I do recall, and what stands out in my mind is that this man always struck me as a gentleman. That lawyer happened to live in our neighborhood and also happened to be our representative in the city council. He later went on to become a judge in the Circuit Court of Cook County and then a Justice on the Illinois Appellate Court.

Looking back, these were likely the initial seeds of my becoming a Family Law lawyer. Years later, when he was a judge and I was a first-year law student, I reached back out to that gentleman about becoming his judicial clerk after my first year of law school. He graciously obliged. During this time I got to observe divorce trials put on by some of the top Family Law attorneys in Chicago. Some of these individuals would later become my colleagues, partners and friends.

I'm often asked the question, why Family Law? I've had other lawyers suggest to me that my talent could be put to better use in some other area of law – perhaps representing some multinational corporation. I cannot think of an area of law where one can have a more meaningful impact on a client's day-to-day life. This is a very solemn responsibility, and one that I take very seriously. The decisions made in domestic relations court e.g., who is awarded the marital home, who will have residential custody of a child, whether one spouse has to pay another spousal support and how retirement assets are divided have very real consequences for not only the parties, but the children involved. This is why I choose Family Law.

What are your final thoughts for working professionals who want to achieve a smooth and seamless transition to the next chapter of their lives?

I often see pro se litigants (litigants who represent themselves) in Family Law court. People choose to represent themselves for a number of reasons: they don't trust lawyers; they feel that their case is simple enough that legal representation is not needed; and often they simply cannot afford a lawyer.

The first issue – trust, may be the most difficult to address and to overcome. You should interview more than one attorney prior to hiring a lawyer to handle your divorce or other Family Law matter. People have an innate sense of things like genuineness and authenticity.

When you interview a lawyer, there are guideposts that you can look for to help you determine whether a potential attorney is someone that you believe trustworthy. Does he or she seem to have a genuine interest in your issues? Are they attentive and thoughtful? Do they seem to provide honest feedback and analysis?

I often admonish my clients that it is not my job to tell them what they want to hear, but what they need to hear. If you hang up the phone or leave a consultation meeting with any reservation at all about the possible lawyer, trust your gut - do not hire them. When you hire a Family Law attorney, you are entrusting someone with the disposition of your income, property and children – make sure that it is someone you can trust.

The second issue I believe is wrapped in hubris. I'd like to think that I am a reasonably intelligent person, but I would rather not try to change the brake pads on my car simply because it is a relatively routine job. No matter how simple you believe the issues in your case are, you are not a lawyer. After almost a decade of practicing law, I continue to learn new things almost every day. If you have never practiced law, you cannot begin to fathom how much you don't know about Family Law specifically and the practice of law in general. If you have the resources to hire an attorney, do not try to handle your case on your own just because your case is "simple" and you believe that you can. I have observed Family Law practitioners fail to properly prepare motions, poorly draft agreements and worse, leave important provisions out of settlement agreements. It is unlikely that you will fare better as a non-lawyer.

Finally, there are those who do not hire counsel because they are unable to afford legal representation. Fortunately, there are a number of resources out there for litigants who have limited financial resources to obtain counsel. Many state and local governments maintain legal clinics that provide legal representation for low-income individuals in matters such as civil rights, employment, housing and matrimonial law. In addition to these legal aid clinics, many law schools have legal clinics where law students, under the supervision of law professors and/or practicing attorneys, provide legal representation. In Chicago, there are a number of law school clinics that have built fine reputations for providing representation in Family Law matters.

I believe that having competent counsel is vital no matter how large or small your marital estate and how simple or complex the issues in your case. Do not let any of the aforementioned perceived obstacles be an impediment to you obtaining competent counsel. Your money, your property and your children may be at stake. If you want to successfully navigate the divorce/reorganization process, you owe it to yourself to obtain competent legal representation.

What's the easiest way to connect with you?

I am a Family Law attorney. I am not a proponent of divorce. I am a husband and a father and believe very much in the institution of marriage and the benefit to children of intact families. Deciding whether to dissolve your marriage or fight for it is a very serious and intensely personal decision. If you are contemplating divorce, I think the first step in the process should be to have an honest conversation with yourself to decide whether your marriage is irreparably damaged and irretrievably broken. If you do ultimately decide that dissolving your marriage is in your best interest and/or the best interest of your family, the next step is to seek competent, qualified, experienced Family Law counsel.

After someone has made the decision to dissolve their marriage, I am available to them for a free initial consultation. During this initial consultation, we discuss the circumstances that lead them down the path of divorce, background information about themselves and their spouse and their concerns and objectives for their divorce.

If you are pursuing a divorce, are seeking child support or child support modification, are seeking to establish or modify parental responsibility (custody) or parenting time or are headed into marriage and simply want to protect your assets and/or income with a premarital agreement, I can be reached for a consultation at (312)621-5253. The divorce process does not have to be the bitter death of a chapter of your life; instead, it is a restructuring or reorganization of your life.

Things will look a little different or perhaps starkly different than before and this may be painful. However, this can be mitigated if you do the divorce process the right way. This begins with finding the right lawyer. If you take anything from this chapter, I hope that you have gleaned that it is the decisions that you make immediately before, during and after your divorce that determine whether you can seamlessly transition to this next chapter in your life.

BRAD M. MICKLIN, ESQ.

Managing Member of the Micklin Law Group, LLC

Email: Brad@MicklinLawGroup.com

Website: http://www.MicklinLawGroup.com

LinkedIn: Linkedin.com/company/The-Micklin-Law-Group

Facebook: Facebook.com/BradM.MicklinEsq

Twitter: https://twitter.com/BradMicklin

Call: (973)562-0100 - **Text:** (973)970-5032

Brad is the lead attorney and managing member at The Micklin Law Group, LLC. For more than 20 years, he has helped clients through some of the toughest, most emotional experiences in their lives, including in high conflict divorces, child custody battles and probate litigation. He has extensive experience in the courtroom and has gained additional expertise and knowledge through advanced family law courses and training in handwriting analysis, body language and advanced micro expression.

When representing clients involved in difficult family legal matters, Brad makes sure he takes as much time as each client needs to discuss concerns, hopes and fears. From there, he tailors his services to match overarching goals and budgets. He also offers his time, articles and other resources to continually teach his clients about the law, even after representation is over. He even holds client dinners and other events.

Based on his work as a litigator, Brad has earned numerous successful results, including successfully arguing the lead case in New Jersey divorce law defining the laws concerning limited duration alimony and its modification. In addition to his litigation and negotiation experience, Brad also has extensive training and experience in the alternative dispute resolution (ADR) processes. After serving as a mediator for the Attorney General's Office in Delaware, he received certification as a mediator through the Superior Court of New Jersey. He later received an invitation to serve as a commercial arbitrator from the Assignment Judge, Union County, New Jersey.

Brad is originally from Philadelphia, PA, and is a graduate of Temple University and Widener University of Law. When he isn't helping clients, you'll find him playing the guitar, swimming or lifting weights.

HOW FATHERS USE NEW LAWS TO GET CUSTODY OF THEIR CHILDREN
By Brad M. Micklin, Esq.

Describe the clients you work with and the types of situations they find themselves in when they come to you for your help?

I help middle-aged men with custody battles to get equal physical custody and help them enjoy uninterrupted parenting time with their children.

What common obstacles prevent middle-aged men with custody issues from getting equal physical custody and uninterrupted time with their children?

The first common obstacle for middle aged men seeking custody is discouragement. Many are discouraged by the relationship with the mother. Their history in court or discussions they've had with friend's family and peers they often fail to realize. Each case is significantly different, and one should not rely upon the stories of another or even the history of the case as laws are progressively changing.

The second common obstacle is uncertainty with regard to planning custody matters typically involve expert witnesses' counselors, therapists and family doctors quite often middle aged men with custody issues have not been involved with these people. And in these processes or appointments and have difficulty obtaining the information.

The last obstacle is concerns about funding because the litigation can be expensive and often requires expert witnesses which tend to increase costs. Middle aged men with custody disputes are often overly concerned about the costs before they obtain the actual information regarding them.

How would you go about helping your clients to overcome those obstacles, and what kind of results were you able to gain for them?

There are many ways to overcome these issues. The most important is adequate planning.

Middle aged men with custody issues need to be instructed how to obtain information from their family doctors pediatricians and other professionals engaged with the family. They need to meet with not only the individuals involved with their family but interview other fact and expert witnesses along with additional professionals such as custody evaluators and professional therapists to best prepare for any custody dispute.

Lastly, they need to interview these professionals to ensure they are all adequately matched for the issues. The father will have.

Typical results received in a case where there is adequate preparation and is shared equal physical time. New Jersey laws have progressively changed and the traditional custody arrangements where the mother would Tecta typically have primary residence and the father have an alternating weekend has been significantly altered in favor of an equal shared physical custodial arrangement.

What common myths/misconceptions that the people you serve may have about achieving their desired outcome?

The most common misconceptions are men don't get physical custody the s cost of fighting for custody is too great and the negative effects of parental alienation cannot be reversed.

What unknown pitfalls should the reader be aware of?

One of the most common pitfalls or mistakes fathers make while seeking custody is inadvertently causing trauma to their children. Any father seeking to obtain custody or parenting time should avoid actions that are likely to lead to a traumatic experience. For instance fathers should avoid calling the police to enforce parenting time obligations when the children are around. Additionally they should avoid talking negatively about the other parent to that child as well as avoiding all discussions of litigation thereby avoiding involving the child at all.

The second most common mistake middle aged men seeking custody make is hiring a general practice attorney while most attorneys will be versed in custody law. It takes a. Specialist with a concentrated experience in family law and custody to have an in-depth knowledge of the intricate laws as well as the delicate emotions. You need an expert to balance these competing issues.

What are their most common fears about even attempting to achieve their desired outcome?

The most common fear is loss of custody entirely. Many middle aged men with custody disputes fear bringing the issue to court for fear of retaliation from the natural mother that may further alienate or eliminate his current custody and parenting time arrangements.

The second most common fear is the displaced belief that he will be unable to afford the litigation and have to surrender and forfeit his rights in court.

It sounds obvious, but why would your clients want to achieve this outcome?

The main reason or motivation middle aged men would seek custody is ignoring the issue often causes its perpetuation children experience the absence of one parent and often attribute the breakdown in relationship to themselves. This misplaced belief of the child can be quite traumatic. Leading to emotional upset and a further break in the custodial relationship with his or her father.

What led you to this field?

I was drawn to family law and father's rights litigation because my family went through a traumatic divorce which resulted in troubled relationships between me and my siblings and our father. At that time in the 1980's, the laws were not prepared to address custody and parenting problems in the same manner that courts today address them.

Then, as the years progressed, and I became an attorney, I found I had a natural pull towards concentrating my law practice into divorce, family and custody issues. I found I had a great temperament for the emotional difficulties my clients were experiencing, and a compassion dedicated to helping them through such difficult and challenging matters.

Then, in 2010, I found myself in the middle of my own high-conflict divorce. This was probably one of the greatest lessons of all. Up to this time, I had passionately represented my clients without the benefit of truly understanding how it felt on the other side of my conference table; meaning, I was helping my clients but could not fully and completely appreciate their struggle. This changed as I went through my 3-year, high-conflict divorce. I, now, can say that I completely understand what my clients are experiencing that knowledge may be even more powerful than all of my decades of experience.

What are your final thoughts for the reader who wants to get equal physical custody and uninterrupted time with their children?

We concentrate in men's and father's rights. This gives us greater insight into the needs wants and issues facing our clients and makes us uniquely positioned to help them advance their goals and obtain custody of their children. We have insight into specific laws necessary to protect them from loss resulting from loss or changes in employment and modifications of support and, in terms of custody agreements, we successfully implement restraining relocation and preserving their rights to see changes in custody in the future.

If the reader wants to know more, how can they connect with you?

We have a wealth of resources available to fathers seeking custody that you can access and download at http://www.micklinlawgroup.com/divorce-for-men/mens-complex-custody-issues/

If you or someone you know is facing a custody issue or challenge, the best thing they can do is give me a call at (973)562-0100 and mention this book for a free consultation.

In an emergency, should me their name, number and short description of the nature of the emergency to my cell phone at (973)970-5032.

MARIBETH BLESSING, ESQUIRE

Attorney and Sole Owner of: Law Offices of Maribeth Blessing LLC Maribeth Blessing Mediation & Arbitration LLC

Email: mblessing@mbfamilylaw.com

Website: https://www.mbfamilylaw.com

Blog: https://www.mbfamilylaw.com/blog

Twitter: http://www.twitter.com/mblesslaw

Avvo Attorney Profile: Maribeth Blessing

LinkedIn: Law Offices of Maribeth Blessing LLC

Call: (215)-663-9016

Maribeth Blessing concentrates her law practice in family law.

Although recognized as an accomplished litigator and selected by the Judges as a Special Master and Guardian Ad Litem, Maribeth specializes in settling cases outside of a courtroom. She is a leading expert in alternative dispute resolution processes including but not limited to mediation, arbitration, and collaborative family law.

Maribeth has served on Montgomery County, Pennsylvania's Advisory Panel for the Court Conciliation Program since its inception in 1999 and has been the liaison between the Pennsylvania Family Law Section and Children's Rights Committee for years.

Maribeth is a member of numerous alternative dispute institutions including being an Advanced Practitioner with the Association of Conflict Resolution, a practicing member of the International Association of Collaborative Professionals, and the Association of Family and Conciliation Courts.

She is also one of the founders of CPR (Center for Peaceful Resolution) featuring lawyers with "heart" focused on helping families maintain relationships while navigating a divorce.

Maribeth has been recognized yearly as one of Pennsylvania's Super Lawyers as featured in Pennsylvania and Delaware "Super Lawyer" Magazines and as a top attorney in Pennsylvania in Philadelphia Magazine's edition of Super Lawyers.

She has been designated as one of the 10 Best Attorneys in Pennsylvania by the American Institute of Family Law Attorneys consistently since 2014.

She was featured on the Channel 6, ABC nightly news and in the March 2007 issue of Philadelphia Magazine, in the article, "The Divorce Posse". Maribeth also received the distinguished honor of being the recipient of Widener University's School of Law's Alumni Service Award.

Recently, Maribeth was featured on award-winning Impact Makers Radio, in a segment titled, "Let's Talk Divorce".

She advised listeners as to how to choose the right attorney and the right process that would help divorcing couples work together in a peaceful environment to fashion a settlement suited to their needs. She pointed out the benefits of family friendly processes available at a much more economical cost than litigation which leaves couples polarized, traumatized, and financially distraught.

THE CIVIL RESOLUTION TO DISSOLUTION
By Maribeth Blessing

Describe the clients you work with and the types of situations they find themselves in when they come to you for your help?

I help separating parties resolve their legal disputes peacefully and economically, so they can reach a settlement that works for everyone. They work at dissolving a marriage, or a relationship while preserving family unity.

People come to me for help at different stages of separation. Some come for advice as to how to plan for separation and what the implications and ramifications may be as to their legal rights and responsibilities. Others come bewildered, hurt, and lost, having been blindsided by a partner leaving the relationship.

Some clients come disgruntled and wanting to escape the grueling and bitter battle begun in a courtroom that is draining them emotionally and financially. Some are coming after a divorce or a prior settlement to make some changes in their parenting schedule, or adjust the amount of support, or enforce the terms of a Property Settlement Agreement.

Some come angry looking for revenge; others distraught looking for reconciliation; and others anxious to get the whole ordeal behind them with as little damage as possible. But most come confused and seeking the quickest, least painful, and least expensive way to end a relationship or a dispute with dignity intact, maintain the ability to be with their children, and receive their "fair share" of the assets or help in distributing and relieving the debt.

I assist them in finding the right process to meet their goals, their emotional needs, and their wallets. In short, I help them resolve the past, deal with the present, and look forward to the future.

What common obstacles prevent separating parties from resolving their legal disputes peacefully and economically?

The most common and largest obstacle for separating parties who wish to resolve their legal disputes peacefully and economically is the fact that separation and divorce issues are emotionally traumatizing from the inception, - no matter what process is chosen. Setting aside their anger, their grief, fears, insecurities, sense of loss, despair, frustration, to deal with the nuts and bolts of the finances is challenging and sometimes an impossibility. The Courtroom has no time to deal with the emotional aspects of a separation. Family friendly divorce processes do.

Another obstacle is a lack of understanding of any of the processes coupled with the misguidance of family and friends. Nuisance backseat drivers are nothing compared to the plethora of would be divorce experts and backyard advice. Family and friends have good intentions when sharing their divorce war stories and pearly words of wisdom, but more damage is done in establishing false expectations and unrealistic goals for the newly separated. The fires of divorce and separation are fueled, not extinguished.

People are led to believe that their "day in court" will bring them justice and vindication and are fearful of testing a process where there is dignity and respect for one another rather than hatred. Courtroom settings are limited in the issues judges can address in a system that cannot cater to the needs of everyone.

Parties are literally asking a black robed stranger to settle their futures in an adversarial setting which rests on the credibility of the parties. People lie, and everyone loses, - especially children. Justice and fairness are not the hallmarks of a courtroom, which handles each issue in a fragmented rather than global manner. Once you enter a courtroom, the more likelihood is that you will become a high conflict court case and never move on from your dispute and enjoy life again.

The better way is a civil divorce or separation where professionals help in a creative problem-solving environment with the engagement of a team of professionals and clients working together. It can be as simple and economic as cooperative or collaborative attorneys jointly helping the parties navigate the issues and make wise decisions. Depending on the complexity of the case, resolution can be attained through the self-direction of the parties themselves, working through a neutral and well-trained mediator. Another option is good old-fashioned kitchen table discussions after direction and knowledge gained from interfacing with the parties' respective attorneys and a check back to make sure all bases have been covered.

A third obstacle is the internet. While education and exploration are a good thing, reliance on internet information can be counterproductive and even detrimental. People looking for friendly and economic divorces/separations often mistakenly download "do-it-yourself" documents from the internet and try to get through the court system without the benefit of good counsel as to legal rights and responsibilities, which only a competent attorney can provide. Once parties overlook an important asset, such as a retirement account, or fail to consider the availability of financial support, there is no going back to recapture those items once a divorce is final. Penny wise and dollar foolish can create years of regret and heartache.

Good legal counsel is a must, which brings us to another obstacle. It is wise to do one's homework in selecting the appropriate attorney to help one navigate the divorce process and to explore all available divorce and separation options so that your goals and needs can be met. Uncle John, who may practice law in the personal injury field, is not the optimum choice. Look closely at curriculum vitae on websites for a concentration in family law, continued legal education and training to stay abreast of the changes in the law and dispute resolution processes. Make sure your chosen lawyer has the adequate training to offer dispute resolution processes. In addition to my legal educational training, my educational background includes extensive training in the practice of mediation, arbitration, parent coordination, cooperative, and collaborative family law. Look for leadership, awards, recognition, community and professional involvement, and participation in associated affiliations and organizations. Pay attention to referrals and especially to testimonials.

Above all, research their reputation in the legal community and interview several lawyers to make sure you have a good fit and feel confident with your lawyer. Make sure the lawyer is responsive and helps you to make good decisions by laying out your choices and providing you with the tools and legal information necessary to help you understand the repercussions of those decisions.

How have you helped separating parties to overcome those obstacles, and what kind of results were you able to gain for them?

People usually come to me from four sources - (1) via reputation and the experiences of former clients; (2) from their internet research and locating me on Google, FindLaw or my website - www.mbfamilylaw.com; (3) from the recommendations of other lawyers from all fields; (4) from the recommendation of Judges or the Bar Association.

Once a client or mediation couple enters my office, they immediately know they are "home". Mine is not a sterile office, but a warm and welcoming center for education and collaborative work. My office family works as a team and we all stay on top of each and every case. I am responsive to my clients and readily available to them if I am in my office and get back to them by the end of the evening if they have left a message and needed more information than my staff could provide. I am available to them 24/7.

My consultations are educational and thorough and can last in excess of two hours for a nominal flat fee. The preparation begins before clients even attend a consultation as they come with as much information they can gather per my instructions and conversations with them prior thereto. I have already spent a great deal of time with them on the telephone before they schedule the more formal consultation. Parties come to me already confident in my ability to help them. At the initial consultation, we will explore their expectations, needs and goals. No question or concern is overlooked, and they are encouraged to ask questions throughout their relationship with me. Every dispute resolution process is thoroughly discussed with handouts and websites provided for further exploration.

At a consultation or initial mediation session we go through their documents together and begin to strategize the best and most economical way to approach their case. We review their financial documents, assess the assets and debts that are marital or from the relationship and their impact on them in how they may be distributed. We look at budgets and Guidelines. We discuss other professionals that may be helpful in doing necessary valuations of retirement accounts or appraisals of property.

If the collaborative law process is appealing to the client, we discuss what the collaborative team may be that will be helpful to them in their situation. Sometimes, if we have all of the financial information, we may discuss different settlement proposals to discuss with their spouse or partner in hopes of achieving a fair and amicable resolution with "kitchen table" discussions. From the moment a client or mediation couple walk through the door, they become part of our office family and an active participant in resolving their separation issues.

There are no surprises in my practice. Any and all documents or correspondence or communication with Counsel or any other professional involved in the case is shared with our clients as they unfold. The clients or mediating parties are part of the team and always in the loop. Every meeting follows an agenda in which they have participated in fashioning and is followed up with a written summary for their reference and review. Knowledge is power, and understanding is crucial to a client's ability to make informed choices. I am with them every step of the way, and see my role as guidance, not dictatorship.

The more options and creativity I can provide for my clients, with their input and, where possible, the input and creativity of my colleagues, the more choices become available. Everyone leaves the relationship with their needs having been met, more clarity as to the needs of the other party, and a commitment to continued cooperation in fostering the best interests of their family. Better communication is a natural outgrowth of the civil divorce or resolution experience.

Another way in which I help parties meet their goals for a peaceful and economic separation or divorce is to keep the case moving and on track. It is so easy for parties to procrastinate and lose momentum. I ensure that there is cooperation in sharing documents and will immediately contact opposing counsel for an agreement to exchange necessary documents without the necessity of formal and costly discovery requests. Full disclosure is one of the hallmarks of both collaborative law and mediation. So much money and time is wasted in litigation and game playing.

I keep realty checking with my clients and keep them focused on the issues that will set them free as opposed to the emotional issues that can bog them down for their lifetime. Note that alternative dispute resolution processes leave room for the emotional growth as well as the practical and financial growth issues, unlike a court which only has time for the basic issues without the emotion. As a mediator, I often sit in the middle of the conflict and help the parties "walk through the fire" to a place of clarity and peace. Once we have moved through the emotional issues, sometimes with the help of a team member who may be a divorce coach, a child specialist or simply a private therapist, the rest unfolds rather easily. But emotions cannot be ignored, or the parties will get stuck in an emotional quagmire and unable to see the forest for the trees.

So often in separation, parties are in different emotional stages. The party who wants out has had a long time to think about it and plan for it. The "blind sighted" party needs the time to accept the reality of the situation and move through the stages of grief. Dispute resolution processes allow for that emotional equalization, but Courts cannot. My clients set the timing of the divorce process and their needs are paramount, but if they get "stuck" or become their own worst enemy entrenched in the anger and vengeful aspects of separation, I am with them every step of the way to help them move forward and embrace life once again.

Reality checking is vital to keep parties moving forward, as well as drilling down to the real issues that lie beneath the surface. For example, I once had a party in a mediation case who refused to sell the marital home. The parties spent a great deal of time in exploring whether or not either of them could afford to purchase the home from the other, or whether they could afford to keep the marital home until the last child was finished high school.

After looking at every option and using professionals to help the parties understand that this strategically simply could not happen given their financial wherewithal, they both conceded that the house had to be sold. But husband still refused to cooperate in getting it on the market. With much more discussion and working together, it finally came out that Husband's reluctance to sell was that once the house was gone, there would be no place for Wife to return should she decide to reconcile at a later date. Once Husband had an opportunity to work through those feelings with the right professional, the parties were able to get the house on the market in time for a spring sale.

Another very high-income case in the litigation arena was on the brink of settlement but got stalemated when the parties both wanted the lost teeth of their two grandchildren which had been saved in a special box over the years. The respective attorneys met with the parties to show them how much they were spending in legal fees to address this bone of contention and how much more they would spend if they let their "deal" go over this one issue and litigated the entire case. When reality set in, they were able to sit down at a four-way meeting and split the teeth with one getting the first tooth of the oldest child and the other the first tooth of the youngest. They each purchased a new special box and the other was donated to a thrift shop.

What common misconceptions do the separating parties you help have about resolving legal disputes?

One common misconception is that the Court will render justice and resolve all of their legal disputes. Unfortunately, nothing is further from the truth. Family Courts have come a long way over the years and have been more sensitive to the fact that in family law, they are dealing with good people acting at their worst as opposed to criminal law dealing with bad people acting at their best. Although there is now a family bench in most of the Pennsylvania counties where there is more than one or two judges for all types of cases, the system is still fragmented.

There are basically three tracts - support, custody, and equitable distribution of assets and debts. In each tract there are a series of adjudicators with opportunities for settlement, usually comprised of two to three levels - Hearing Officers, Masters/Senior Officers who are attorneys, and then the assigned judge who may rotate off periodically depending on the county, so there is no guarantee of one judge per family. There is no mixing of support, custody and equitable distribution so global settlements are impossible, and oftentimes, the issues attendant to each are interrelated.

The Courts deal with isolated issues, usually one or two related issues within a tract at a time. There are usually court lists so one could be waiting all day to be heard by a judge after exhausting all of the steps to go up the ladder to see a judge. Additionally, most counties have put in place mediation and parenting programs in the custody arena which each having a significant cost.

So, all along the continuum one's wallet is emptied, precious time is wasted, and all for the opportunity to slam the other party and hope for a "win" on that issue, which rarely happens. On top of that, many judges despise family law and would much rather be in criminal or civil court following the Rules of Evidence to a "t" rather than weighing through the emotional separation or divorce issues and dealing with angry and vindictive people.

My peaceful practice allows for global settlement with dignity, understanding, and knowledge and with lots of patience. Global settlements are the norm and the goal. Five-year litigation cases get done in a matter of months with creative solutions and the best use of resources. Why pay for two experts to battle it out in a courtroom when a business needs to be valued? Why not conserve resources and the money for distribution between the separating parties instead of hiring battling "big gun" lawyers and experts who fuel the flames rather than put out the fires?

The opposite of the long dragged out court battle is the "quickie" divorce which is just as lethal. Separating and divorcing couples fall prey to the "one stop shops" or the internet fixes. They mistakenly think they can use "self-help" and save a ton of money, which ends up costing them twice as much if the mistakes they made can even be undone by an attorney at a later date. Putting a band-aid on a wound that needs the skills of a competent surgeon can lead to the loss of a body part. Why would you use a paralegal to draft documents for you or your best buddy or use an internet form that may not be accepted by the Court? Lawyers are legal surgeons and equally educated. They know all of the nuances of the counties in which they practice. They know the judges and their values. They know the law and all of the pitfalls.

Once I had an accountant brag to me as to how he helped a couple resolve their property distribution issues and file their own divorce papers. "It was simple", he said. Husband had a retirement account that was worth the same as the marital home. Wife wanted the retirement account; Husband wanted the home, so they agreed to swap, and so didn't need to go through the expense of having a Property Settlement Agreement that would be incorporated in their divorce decree, to be drafted by a reviewing attorney.

A reviewing attorney might have told them that it was not an "equal" swap as the retirement account had tax consequences and the home could be liquidated for its cash value. The accountant told them that they could just file the paperwork for a simple decree and then swap out the property - or so he thought.

So, they did, and soon learned that Wife couldn't just transfer her share of the marital home to Husband, as there was nothing she could do about getting her name off the mortgage for which she continued to be liable, unless refinance was dictated in a Property Settlement Agreement. Oh, but there wasn't one! And on top of that, she couldn't get his retirement account because it was governed by ERISA federal law which required a special document called a Qualified Domestic Relations Order that had to be specifically mentioned in a Property Settlement Agreement so that the retirement account could be transferred to Wife without immediate income tax repercussions or penalty.

Oh no, there wasn't a Property Settlement Agreement! So, Husband had to cash in his retirement account to give to Wife. But he wasn't fifty-nine and one half, so he also had to pay a 30% penalty plus income taxes on the amount taken.

Wife did not get the full amount of retirement rollover for which she bargained, and the mortgage company would not allow the deed transfer to Husband without the payoff of the mortgage so they both lost. The Decree had been issued without a Property Settlement Agreement. It would take some legal maneuvering to attempt to get permission from the Court to allow for a vacate of the decree and a Property Settlement Agreement to be properly drawn up to fix this mess - very expensive with no guarantee of success. If the Court said "no", then you have two ruined lives. Hope that accountant had lots of professional malpractice insurance and realized that he held himself open for criminal sanctions for the unauthorized practice of law!

Some go for the advertised "cheap" divorces where some lawyers file a divorce in a county which has minor filing fees of maybe $50 versus $400 dollars. What they don't tell you is that counties that do so and allow filings where the parties reside outside of that county, will only handle uncontested divorces with no property, support or custody issues. So, what happens when the decree comes down and you ask for your share of the pension you knew your spouse had? The answer is "tough - you snooze, you lose".

When divorce settlements are going to set the tone for the rest of your lives, why would anyone not seek the advice of an expert who practices family law on a daily basis and knows the pitfalls? I doubt if you would take your million-dollar lottery winnings to the casino and bet number 9 when you can get legal or investment advice on how to turn that million into two million! And what happens if you divorced in one of those counties and then learned that your spouse made three times as much as you and since you were married thirty years, you missed out on an alimony award that could have been for ten or more years at 40% of the difference of your net incomes? Oh well - gone in sixty seconds and hindsight is 20-20! And if there is a parenting dispute, guess what?

You are still going to have to file for custody where the children reside, and the filing fees are almost as much as a divorce filing. Had you filed for divorce in your own county at the inception, you would only be looking at a nominal fee to add a custody count.

But consider this. If you had done your homework out of the gate and researched a competent attorney who is knowledgeable in alternative dispute resolution processes, you could have reached a global settlement with your spouse or partner, preserved the family relationship while dissolving the marriage or relationship, covered all of your legal bases, and maintained your sanity and your wealth. You could have saved enough in legal fees to put all of your kids through college! And on top of that, maintain your dignity and develop a new trust and respect for the other parent/party which can only benefit you and your children. And the icing on the cake is that you have developed a new and better way of communicating. Why not consider the civil resolution to separation and move ahead with no regrets as to how you handled the dissolution of your relationship?

What are unknown pitfalls should your clients be aware of when looking for a peaceful and economic dissolution of their relationship?

Avoid one-stop-shops! There are all kinds of innovative get rich quick one-stop-shops that border on the unauthorized practice of law and propose to save you money. In the long run, they may cost you a fortune. One such type is paralegals setting up shops to "draft" your divorce documents. First of all, they may be competent to draft documents for a lawyer's review and modification, but usually not independently. They avoid scrutiny as you pay a fee and they "ghost write" your documents as though you, yourself drafted them. They may even go so far as to tell you how to file them. Other than a competency issue, another problem is that each county has their own nuances in the drafting and filing of documents. They are not uniform documents.

For example, in Montgomery County, Pennsylvania, if you want Domestic Relations (the first stop of the support tract) to consider alimony *pendente lite* as well as spousal support, you must first file it as a count in the divorce complaint and then refile the divorce complaint in Domestic Relations. This can become vital and necessary in the event there is an entitlement contest on the spousal support. Spousal support is designed to help the dependent spouse with household expenses, so if the dependent spouse has committed marital misconduct such as infidelity during the marriage, an entitlement issue can be raised to prevent him/her from getting spousal support.

Alimony *pendente lite* is the same dollar amount under the Guidelines and is intended to equalize the parties financially so that there is no disadvantage in litigating a divorce. There can be no entitlement issue raised. So, if there is a danger one won't get support because of marital misconduct, you certainly would want a backup theory where there is no entitlement issue!

That is information only a well-versed attorney would know, and not the paralegal who won't tell you how to file documents in each separate county. Oh, and by the way, that whole system may change shortly as there are new proposed rules to civil procedure, that, if passed will require all support filings to go through Domestic Relations and not be included in a divorce complaint. Only an attorney on top of their game would have such knowledge. So, if you trust the blind leading the blind, go ahead and throw away your money and create a legal nightmare. Please don't be penny wise and dollar foolish! Seek out the attorney!

Another one-stop shop that is cropping up is the Arbitration "fix". For the total sum of $8,000-$15,000 for both spouses, you can go to a place where a panel of two to three lawyer arbitrators will take all of your financial information, and without a formal hearing, come back and tell you how to divide your property and set your alimony in a binding legal document. Then the staff paralegals will draft all of your documents for you to file on your own to process your decree as though you never entered their doors. Quick? Definitely! Fair? Maybe, but probably not. Economical? Maybe, depending on the size of your marital estate. Appealable if you don't like the outcome? No!

Then there is the mediation "mill". For a retainer of $7500-$1200 dollars you go to one of the organization's mediators, who sometimes literally advises you how to divide your assets, your kids, and your money. Mediators who are not lawyers should not be providing legal advice. The damage that is done by such a practice is devastating.

Even if they are lawyers, as a lawyer/mediator, I think it borders on the unethical as you are acting as a neutral mediator, not as a lawyer in an adversarial practice. In these "mills", a real lawyer then reviews the Mediator's Memorandum and drafts the Property Settlement Agreement for the parties, but usually never really meets the parties, as in Pennsylvania, no lawyer may represent both parties in an adversarial proceeding such as a divorce. Then a paralegal again ghost writes all of the divorce documents except the Agreement (which is rarely reviewed by an unbiased lawyer for each side but should be!). The parties file their own documents. I wonder how they decide who should be the Plaintiff and who should be the Defendant? That alone is laden with potential problems.

I have been the reviewing lawyer on a number of these Agreements and almost always find that something really big was either missed completely or handled incorrectly leaving the parties vulnerable for major litigation in the future. Besides, I get offended at the outrageous flat fee expense for this type of "service". Parties who mediate in my office will pay far less. It would take 10 sessions with me to make the base retainer of a "mill", and it is rare that parties need more than four or five sessions of mediation and more often require only two to three sessions because they come prepared to mediate and with all documents in tow. You do the math. Don't be suckers for the fast deal. If it sounds too good to be true, it probably is!

What are their most common fears about even attempting to resolve their legal disputes peacefully and economically, so they can reach a settlement that works for everyone?

Here are some of the most common fears:

"My spouse can't be trusted." Let's think about this one. You married or lived with and trusted this person from the onset. You may have borne children together out of that initial love. That person has been your partner, your confident, and your protector until things went awry in your relationship. People grow apart for various reasons, but that doesn't mean they stop being a good person. These alternative dispute resolution processes rebuild the trust with guidance from the professionals involved. Your attorney still has your back, but helps you find a peaceful way of having meaningful discussions as to your needs, your spouse's needs and your family's needs. Everyone works together to develop the best plan for continuing to parent and nurture your children together, for making sure everyone's financial needs are covered, and to fairly distribute your assets and liabilities. If the chosen process is mediation, make sure you still have the benefit of an attorney to educate you on the legal rights and responsibilities of both spouses, and provide you legal advice every step of the way as you work independently with your spouse through the mediation process. Everything you do or buy in your lifetime, requires careful thought, research and planning. Why would you jump into a mediation where your decisions determine your future, or even litigation without the guidance and expertise of a lawyer?

"I don't know anything about our finances. My spouse always paid the bills and controlled the money." All the more reason to consider an alternative resolution process! In both mediation and collaborative family law, there is an inherent duty to provide full disclosure. If you know nothing about the financial picture, then I recommend the latter process, as you will have your attorney with you every step of the way, and access to other professionals to help to determine the marital estate that is available for distribution.

These professionals know exactly what they need to keep you protected and, in both processes, there is a commitment to willingly share all relevant information. In the court setting, formal discovery is utilized which could comprise Interrogatories, Requests for Production of Documents, Requests for Admissions, Depositions and Subpoenas. Sounds scary? It is! There is no guarantee there will be cooperation in producing the requested discovery and even if produced, whether or not there has been full disclosure. In an adversarial setting, people tend to hide things, and provide as little information as they can. There are Motions to Compel and Motions for Sanctions that can be filed, but if you are doing the math, you will quickly see that your divorce has now become extremely expensive, and frustrating.

"I don't get along with my spouse and can't be alone in the same room with them." Well, the purpose of alternative dispute resolution processes is to provide that opportunity to talk, with the help of professionals who are trained to encourage and support constructive discussion. Who, better than the two of you knows your situation, and is better able to make good decisions as to how you are both going to emotionally and financially survive a divorce or separation?

"My spouse will charmingly manipulate the process and lie, and I will be at a disadvantage." It is not unusual for there to be a power struggle in any separation or divorce. There probably was a constant power struggle through any relationship break up or deterioration. Usually each party sees the other as manipulative and controlling either in a passive aggressive or more volatile manner. That doesn't change whether they are in a court setting or not, and oftentimes an aggressive client teams up with an aggressive lawyer, which means double the intimidation and nastiness.

Power struggles are easily controlled by trained professionals in alternative dispute resolution processes. The mediator or collaborative lawyer has tools in their repertoire that ensure a level "playing field". When the teams of professionals are involved in a collaborative setting, the mental health professional manages the emotions and assists the parties in ensuring their voice is heard. If the team is simply the parties and their lawyers, the collaborative lawyers work together to make sure everyone is heard and provided with the opportunity to participate in all discussions. Before each team meeting, there is preparation with the client and an agenda that has been determined by the team and the parties.

"How are we ever going to be able to afford two houses and how can we share the children when they need one stable home". The first part of that fear is a reality as it is always less expensive for parties to stay in one home and continue to share expenses than to support two homes. The timing of when the actual split will occur and how finances are handled in the interim is often a subject of an early mediation or collaborative meeting for parties who have not yet physically separated. The Court cannot even address the finances until after an actual split. Careful planning of that transition is vital for both the financial and the parenting aspect. That is not a luxury afforded in the court system.

The other reality is that once the split has occurred the children will have two homes, not one. Helping the parties fashion schedules that suit the best interests of the children in terms of stability and continuity in an amicable setting is also crucial as opposed to having a schedule thrust upon them by a judge who knows very little about the parties and does not have the opportunity how this family functions together or not. In the collaborative or mediation processes, the parties can work together to ensure that both homes suit the needs of the children and continue to foster continuity in expectations and routines established during the relationship.

One of my most successful collaborative cases involved a client of mine who knew very little about the intricate finances of the marriage, was extremely anxious and volatile, and who couldn't stand to even look at her husband, whom she found to be passive aggressive at best. At first, I was concerned that she would not be able to trust or handle an intense collaborative meeting. After learning the facts of the case, I quickly realized we would never be able to get the financial information we needed through the court process without spending thousands and thousands of dollars and enduring time delay, and even then, probably would not have it all. Plus, there was a family business involved, a possible criminal case threatening Husband which would severely impact Wife, and marital assets in excess of eight million dollars that could potentially be sucked into the criminal case and lost forever. It would have taken at least five years for this case to get through the court system and we did not have that amount of time to protect the parties. It also would have probably cost the parties in excess of $150,000 each just for basic legal fees, and an additional $50,000 each for the required evaluation experts, by my assessment and that of the collaborative attorney with whom I worked closely.

This case cried out for professional help. So, Counsel, along with the parties, a financial advisor, business expert, and a child specialist/divorce coach worked diligently and had all matters settled within a year, and prior to any criminal action being initiated against Husband by his business siblings. Wife and the children were totally protected, the assets were distributed and out of reach, and the parties were able to continue parenting their children together in a respectful and amicable manner.

There were days when one spouse did not even want to make eye contact with the other, so seating was arranged to accommodate that need and sometimes negotiations took place with the parties in separate rooms and the professionals moving between them. That case may have looked like a case that should go to litigation at the onset and not be able to be handled in a collaborative setting, but as it turned out, it was highly successful and only served to prove that every separating couple should be afforded the opportunity and the support to move through a process that makes them the integral center of the decision-making process. With much creative thinking and cooperation, we all worked together for a comprehensive, creative, and economic resolution.

Our financial advisor even went to one of the properties to help the parties organize an auction, and we helped them find the right professional to materialize the maximum profit on the sale of their antique car collection.

It sounds obvious, but why would your clients want to resolve their dispute peacefully and economically and reach a resolution that works for everyone?

Obviously, anyone would want to choose the divorce process that costs the least as long as it covers all of the bases and results in a fair outcome. The litigation process is most often the most expensive, time-consuming, traumatic and destructive process one can choose. People are never satisfied with decisions that are thrust upon them. Parents are polarized forever and cannot co-parent for the good of their children. Children become embroiled in the trauma and conflict.

The most compelling reason people look to alternative dispute resolution processes is to protect their children and preserve the family unit. Children can be in the court system for eighteen years and there is nothing more heart-wrenching than watching a child being put on a witness stand in front of both of their parents or being interviewed in the judge's chambers. The emotional damage is never cured. Children want parents to stay together. They want to please both parents. Parents need to think about what memories they want to create for their children. The best protection one can give their children is to keep them out of the disputes, keep their best interests forefront in their conversations, and address the children's needs and not the parents' "wants".

Parties can examine each parent's strengths and weaknesses and cover one another. Best of all, parents can maintain unity and structure for the children, and both be present at all of the children's events, thus supporting the children and one another. Studies show that children need both parents, so better that the parents resolve their dispute in a manner that works for everyone and preserves the heart of the family.

Courtrooms bring out the worst in people, who are defensive and fighting hard for what they want. Lawyers are hired as the big guns to get them what they want. It is an adversarial setting where all of the skeletons are dragged out of the closet, and dirty laundry is aired in open court in an effort to convince a black robed third party that you should get what you want because the other party is bad. At the end of the day there is no dignity, no consideration, no justice, and no money. Mediation, Collaborative Family Law, and other dispute resolution hybrids give parties the opportunity to figure things out themselves, with as much professional help as they may need.

It opens the door to better communication, which is oftentimes the reason for the breakup. It explores everyone's needs, and core values, and works toward a resolution where everyone can walk away feeling they have been respectfully treated and heard. It provides opportunities for obtaining clarity in positions or underlying motives, and an opportunity to explore and evaluate and ultimately change focus from the negative to the positive. These processes avoid the trauma of the courtroom, the trickle-down effect on the children, and the wasted time and money. They allow for a global and comprehensive settlement that best meets everyone's goals and needs.

In a peaceful setting, the parties gain knowledge and direction. They explore better ways to manage their monies, and to divide their wealth fairly, as opposed to spending their life savings in a traumatic courtroom setting. The parties receive the benefit of exploring lots of creative ideas coming from one another and the professionals they have chosen who work together and with the parties to navigate and resolve all of their issues. Most of all, parents can move on with their lives, while preserving the family life they established during their relationship as opposed to becoming the high conflict case that is wed to the courtroom for the rest of their children's minority.

What led you to the field of alternative dispute resolution processes?

My love of children culminated in a teaching career which was always my dream. I followed a military Husband and taught all over the United States including Alaska which was the only public school experience I had.

Life is a series of crossroads and choices. There came a time when I had to return to my home state of Pennsylvania and begin raising my children alone as a single mother. I lamented the fact that my children lost a Father who was an integral part of their lives, but he made his choice not to be any longer. I would have given anything for the opportunity to co-parent with him after a divorce that was not nasty, but sudden and quick, and which I didn't see coming.

A kind attorney got me through that ordeal and I vowed I would pay back that favor a hundred-fold. I know how it felt to lose the security of a home and a family unit and to re-enter the world afraid, lonely, and devastated. It was both an emotional and a financial struggle at first, but with a strong faith basis and a supportive family, I picked up the pieces and moved on, opening the next chapter of my life and ready to embrace change.

I found myself working for children in a different way when I became a bench warrant investigator and enforcement officer for delinquent child support offenders. That matriculated into a Hearing Officer conducting support conferences and encouraging litigating parties and their Counsel to reach an amicable settlement that both parties could tolerate. After eight years of watching some attorneys fuel the fires of separation rather than help put out the fires, I decided I needed to do something to change the focus of a separation from a destructive ending to the opportunity for a constructive beginning.

While working as an Officer of the Court, I went to law school nights and upon obtaining my law degree and license, began working and studying with a very prominent family lawyer. I learned how to service my clients well, how to be organized and prepared for court and how to "win" cases and develop a reputation with the court for fairness and professional diligence.

For four years I focused on litigation, but still concentrated on settling cases out of court, which for me, was the real winning case. I then opened a Center for Matrimonial Resolution with another mentor of mine and while maintaining my litigation practice, also focused on moving towards a more peaceful practice. I could not get enough education in this field! I am passionate about the work I do, and every time I help parties obtain a peaceful resolution, it is akin to the joys of new birth.

In 1999 I opened my own firm, with a vow to continue to move towards a peaceful practice. However, I soon realized that I could be more instrumental in helping litigation-oriented parties to find a more peaceful and economical way of moving through the divorce process, and to do so, they sometimes needed a "taste" of the other alternative -litigation. Most people quickly see the light. My litigation practice still remains for those who simply cannot embrace the concept that there is a better way to go through a break up process, but every day my peaceful practice grows, and my litigation practice diminishes. My goal is to move to a solely peaceful practice within two years and let the young litigators in my firm continue the litigation practice, as there will always be unbelievers who insist on doing things the hard way. However, all my attorneys are also well trained in alternative dispute resolution processes and strive to settle cases as opposed to litigating them, even if that must happen on the courthouse steps.

I am extremely active in bringing the mediation and collaborate world to the public through educational programs and it is part of every single consultation that I provide. I find I sleep a lot better at night when a case settles as opposed to litigates and I am positive that my clients do as well.

What are your final thoughts for the reader who wants to know more about finding a more peaceful and economic process for divorce that will result in a resolution that works for everyone?

Divorce or separation is difficult and traumatic. Stay away from litigation that only exacerbates the situation, leaving you emotionally and financially drained. Although there is no guarantee that mediation, collaborative family law, cooperative negotiation, or arbitration will be less expensive, the likelihood is that it will significantly reduce the financial strain.

Refrain from self-help. Cutting out the attorney in your process, whatever it may be, will result in more legal fees in the future to undo what you missed or got wrong. Make sure you obtain legal advice before you initiate ANY process for separation or divorce. It is wise to have an attorney coach if your choice is mediation.

Make sure you have researched and chosen an attorney wisely - one who is well versed in family law, up to date on their education, well respected and known in the field, concentrates their practice in family law, and a good fit with you and your goals. In choosing an alternative dispute resolution process, make sure your advocate has had substantial training in that field, is current in continuing education, active and reputable in their field and a good fit with you and your goals.

Be prepared to free up your schedule and take the time needed to thoroughly address the issues related to your separation or divorce. It is a lifetime investment of time and energy. If you are in the court setting, you must take off from work for numerous court commitments as the court is not going to cater to your schedule or to your emotional state. In other processes, meetings can be scheduled around the availability of everyone. One major advantage to the other resolution processes is that they are far less time consuming and accommodations are made to provide time for you to be ready emotionally and financially to proceed. Don't rush the process. Make sure you cover every item that is important to you. Make your attorney aware as to what you are feeling and what you are thinking. We are your voice in a courtroom, and we make sure your voice is heard at each meeting in a dispute resolution process.

Surround yourself with positive and supportive people when you are going through a separation or divorce. Misery loves company and water seeks its own level. Don't listen to the horror stories or the myriad of bad advice. Only seek the advice of your attorney, weigh it and make your own choices. You get to write your separation story. You get to determine how acrimonious or peaceful the process will be.

Take the time you need to feel and deal. Cry if it helps you. Gather your trusted friends and vent. Take deep breaths and get yourself emotionally and intellectually ready to get down to work and figure out how you want to live the rest of your life. Get help! Engage a therapist to help you get through the grieving process. Divorce is a death - the loss of the "forever and ever" promise. Let yourself feel the pain and move through it.

Don't involve the children! They are not your confident nor your therapist. Remember, while you are dealing with your fears and the loss of a spouse, they are watching their whole world crumble and are fearful of losing both parents. Pay more attention to them. Watch them for signs of anxiety or depression. Get them emotional help to cope if necessary. Keep your spouse aware of their emotional state so you can work together to protect them. Stay positive with them. Remind them daily that they still have two parents who love them dearly. Never bad mouth your spouse within earshot of the children, or at all if you can refrain. Remember that what goes around, comes around. Any attempt at alienating the other parent usually results in you losing the respect and confidence of your children.

Don't be afraid to try another process. Listen to your inner heart and don't worry about what other people say. Nowhere is it written that an ex-spouse has to be your enemy. In fact, people who go through alternative dispute resolution processes often develop a respectful and working relationship to continue co-parenting their children. Even where there are no children, your ex-spouse can still be your friend, or at least a respected co-parent Remember you started in love and respect. The love may be gone, but the respect can be nurtured.

Lose the skepticism. These processes can work for you. Read about them and learn about the benefits. Come committed to success and you will succeed!

If the reader wants to know more, how can they connect with you?

If you or anyone else you know is thinking about a separation, please don't make any changes until you are sure of the changes you want to make and the repercussions of those changes.

It is always best to schedule an informational meeting with an attorney to learn about the do's and don'ts in planning for a separation, and the many processes available to aid you and your spouse along the path of separating your lives.

Should you or someone close to you be the surprised recipient of a request for a divorce or the party left unexpectedly behind, seek the immediate support of loved ones and family.

Once you've dried your eyes or even if still crying, give me a call, as you will need the compassion and understanding of a good attorney with a level head to help you focus on the tasks at hand and pick up the pieces.

My office family will become your family and your support, right down to Zoe, our little Pekingese, who knows how to comfort and love you when you are feeling down.

I am your first source for more information on any and all alternative dispute resolution processes. Feel free to call me at 215 663-9016 and I will be happy to spend whatever time necessary to help you obtain all the information and assurances that you need to consider an amicable and economical separation or divorce.

A second source is my personal website at https://www.mbfamilylaw.com where you will find detailed information and articles as to all of the resolution processes and lots of specific information regarding divorce and separation issues.

You can also enjoy a video of our office family, listen to my radio interview with Impact Makers Radio, a POD presentation on alternative resolution processes, and review many testimonials from my clients and mediating parties.

If you want more information, please feel free to email me at mblessing@mbfamilylaw.com.

You can read about me on AVVO.com or connect with me on LinkedIn or Facebook. And there is always our friend, Google, the eyes and the ears of the internet world.

When you are ready, at your convenience, we will schedule a full informational consultation which usually lasts at least two hours, to ensure you have the opportunity to explore all avenues of divorce or separation processes open to you, and to assess and begin the planning the resolution of your own case.

You will be welcomed to my cozy office and greeted by a furry friend and a smiling receptionist with warm coffee or refreshing water. You will meet your new office family that works as a team to make sure we are always available to you.

This full two-hour consultation is offered at a nominal fee which is less than the hourly rate of any of our attorneys. Any prior support or inquiry telephone calls are free of charge. Hugs are also free and plentiful.

KENDRA THOMAS, ESQ., CFLS

Attorney, Thomas Law Offices, APC

Email: kthomas@law-thomas.com

Website: http://wwww.law-thomas.com

LinkedIn: https://linkedin.com/in/kendrathomas

Facebook: https://facebook.com/ThomasLawOffices

Twitter: https://twitter.com/amazinglawgirl

Avvo Attorney Profile: Kendra Thomas

Call: (877)479-7970

Mediator, Author, Attorney and law firm Founder, Kendra Thomas is a family law practitioner in Southern California. Having offices in Woodland Hills and Newport Beach, Kendra is certified by the State Bar of California as a Certified Family Law Specialist.

Whether inside a courtroom or in mediation, Kendra represents clients in a variety of family law matters ranging from negotiating complicated premarital agreements to straightforward and simple divorce. She has dedicated her career to helping her clients reach their financial and legal goals while transitioning through the most difficult times in their life. She has also provided outside strategic counsel to other top-named divorce attorneys in servicing their high-profile clients.

Kendra's knowledge of custody disputes allows her to litigate both in the Family Law and Dependency Courts. She counsels clients directly in appropriate litigation strategy and how to de-escalate conflict in child custody matters to serve the best interests of their children.

As a passionate award-winning advocate for victims of Domestic Violence, Kendra has been instrumental in teaching and changing the law, serving on many committees to give back to the legal community.

She also opines as a legal expert in newscasts, podcasts and on reality television.

DIVORCING TODAY, PRESERVING ASSETS FOR TOMORROW
By Kendra Thomas

Tell us about Thomas Law Offices, APC, the people you work with and the types of situations they find themselves in when they come to you for your help?

Whether you have a residence, real estate holdings, bank accounts, brokerage accounts and/or retirement accounts, retaining as much of your wealth as possible should be a goal. I help people with assets to retain their resources, so they can rebuild their lives after divorce.

What are the advantages of retaining resources for the people you help?

How you financially come through your divorce can often set the stage for the next stage of your life. The advantage of retaining your resources through your divorce gives you options. The more resource you are able to retain, the more seamless the transition to the next stage of your life. If you had to sell your family residence, you may be able to purchase a new one. If you want to keep the children in the family residence, you may be able to buy your spouse out of their interest. If it is time for your children to go to college, you may be able to offer financial support. If you are close to retirement age, you may still be able to retire on schedule.

What do you feel are the biggest myths out there when it comes to litigating with assets?

There are many myths that come with litigation. The most prevalent being that the court will get into the minutia of your finances in divorce to prevent the spenddown of assets, leaving litigants free to do whatever they would like without it impacting the parties' financial bottom line.

Courts loathe to get involved in private affairs any more than required. The concept that a Judge or the court are going to police your divorce to ensure you financial solvency after divorce is simply false. The courts assume that parties know what is in their own best interests and allow them to make whatever strategic decisions necessary to get them through the process. Generally speaking, absent a request for attorney's fees or some other request that requires the court to look into litigation costs, the court does not concern itself with the expense the parties face as a result of the litigation. This means that there are no preventative measures automatically in place to ensure that assets will not need to be spent down to cover excessive litigation costs.

Many times the out spouse, or the spouse who did not handle the finances during the marriage, does not completely understand the community finances. Without a comprehensive understanding of the finances, this may lead to a belief that the assets are greater than they are or maybe even the perception that they are unlimited or can shoulder whatever the litigation burden. This can drive reckless litigation behavior that can bring ruin upon the community estate. If a court does not deal with this until the time of trial, this means that a Judge may not even have the chance to opine or make a ruling until the community estate is already is shambles.

What are some common misconceptions around the Legal industry?

There are a lot of misconceptions surrounding the legal industry. In the practice of family law, especially, there are a lot of misconceptions about what we do and why we do what we do. Many people feel that since we deal with clients during delicate times in their lives, we should operate from emotion as opposed to business. In the halls of a courthouse or at mediation, I will often hear clients remark that they are annoyed that their attorney is not taking the client's matter as personally as the client is and/or they feel that because this is a difficult time, the attorney should be cutting them a break financially. Although both of these comments are very human, both responses lose sight of the fact that attorneys are professionals and the practice of law is a business. When an attorney is retained, a business relationship with business parameters is created. In its rawest form, a client should receive counsel in exchange for payment.

When you are bogged down with wading through your own emotional and legal turmoil, it is easy to lose sight of your advocate as a person. However, the reality is that at the heart of the business relationship is someone who also has their own life and their own bills to pay. This means that although an attorney can feel bad for their client, there is nothing to be gained by the attorney taking on any personal stake in the client's matter. As emotion increases, logic decreases. Although emotionally you may feel that you are best served by an attorney who is able to commiserate with you emotionally; strategically, you benefit from an attorney who, while empathetic, is able to maintain logic, perspective and a sense of balance in advising you on steering you towards the end goal.

What are some of your client's most common fears about losing their resources?

Understanding your end goal in transitioning through your divorce will allow you to stay the course during this difficult time. As there are many moving parts to settlement and litigation, there are times that the process will force you to face fears -- i.e. the unknowns of litigation, the potential to have to liquidate assets to fund litigation, feeling powerless when the Judge makes an order that makes no financial sense from your perspective.

Most of the aforementioned scenarios, although scary, can be overcome with time. However, the concept of losing one's assets in litigation, either to fund the litigation or in awarding the other party's interests can be more difficult to overcome. The fear of having to give up assets (that it seemingly took a lifetime to accumulate) can be paralyzing and prevent litigants from fully engaging in the process or using any resource to hire a legal advocate. To that end, many times I will see a litigant represent themselves and enter a process that they are not equipped to maneuver alone. This becomes apparent when they cannot understand how they are hit with an award for spousal support or a fee award to opposing counsel that they simply cannot fathom.

Difficult financial orders that appear burdensome and that are not understood can fuel more aggressive litigation as the fear sets in deeper and the litigant is not only faced with the fear of losing everything but not being able to rebuild or get back to where they were prior to the start of the litigation.

What should people with assets do to get past those fears?

The most comforting words a legal advocate can give their client, especially when they are stuck in a fear loop can be -- "it will be okay, you will get through." Although the process of divorce sucks, it is important to realize that this too shall pass. Divorce, like all processes, has a beginning, a middle and an end. Being able to understand that there is an end to the process can keep hope alive even during the darkest times of the process. Focusing on what comes next can also be a useful tool in strategizing through your divorce in a manner that keeps you on track to start the next phase of your life.

How your divorce is strategized can be the difference between being able to walk away with something as opposed to nothing. Working with a knowledgeable advocate and providing them as much information as possible regarding your estates (both community and separate) at the inception of your case can streamline your dissolution process and allow you to stay focused on the end result.

What other perceived obstacles do you see that might be preventing people with assets from seeking the help of an Attorney?

Some clients are reluctant to start their divorce process with an attorney because they are concerned that an attorney will complicate the process. In some respects, that thinking can be correct. Picking an advocate or the wrong advocate can be costly. After all, there is a reason that attorneys have such negative reputations. However, having said that, picking the correct attorney for you can have immeasurable value for your case.

The number one concern I hear from prospective clients who want just a little bit of advice, so they can handle their own matter is that they are afraid that bringing in an attorney will result in invoices they are unable to afford and delays in their case. The reality is that a good advocate will set forth their fee agreement in a retainer agreement that is easy to read and understand. A good attorney will also itemize their billing, so you should know what has happened on your matter and how much you have on retainer with their firm. These basics guide the relationship and ensure that you cannot be financially abused. Additionally, with the right advocate, a strategy can be set from the outset with estimate of the cost, ensuring value and minimizing risk in the litigation.

When it comes to retaining their resources, what are some of the common pitfalls and mistakes you see people make?

The biggest mistake made in litigation is not have a litigation plan. By not having a litigation plan, litigants can get caught up in back and forth of litigation. For every discovery request that is made, it is matched and for every motion that is brought it is fought in the courtroom. This can serve to throw gasoline on the flames of the stoked ligation fire. When litigation is approached through the lens of an eye for an eye, as opposed to performing tasks to move you towards your end goal, that is when resources are wasted. Every step that is initiated on your behalf should move you forward towards the end goal on your litigation plan and/or serve to de-escalate the conflict so out of court resolution is possible.

How can these pitfalls or mistakes be avoided?

If the goal is preservation of resource, fueling litigation with more litigation does not meet that end. Therefore, (1) have a litigation plan that can guide you, (2) try to anticipate what the other side will need through divorce and address it prior to their needing to file a motion, and (3) when served with a motion, try to look for resolution that does not involve additional litigation.

Many issues that are subject to litigation do not come out of thin air. They can be anticipated. I see this a lot in realm of spousal and/or child support. If it is apparent that you or your ex will require support, it may make sense to figure out support and/or make an offer of support instead of needing to litigate the issue. Some take the position that they will not pay anything until a court requires it; however, this can be a stubborn and costly position that could result in the expenditure of extra fees and/or costs that could otherwise be avoided.

Share an example of how you have helped someone to overcome those obstacles and succeed in rebuilding their lives after divorce.

I often see clients getting caught up in litigation to where it is driven by ego and/or emotion. If the other side puts a hearing on calendar than the inclination is that my client wants to put a hearing on calendar. If we have to answer discovery, I will soon face the question "you better make the other side do this too."

In situations wherein, I see multiple hearings that are being continued out and no result is being reached, I will try to get to the bottom of why this has been the strategic history. In many situations I run into litigants who are caught up in litigation because they do not want to appear weak or they are trying to validate some other emotional response. They cannot get out of their own way. When I see this, I have been successful in getting our clients out of their own way by refocusing them on the future. I have saved clients tens of thousands of dollars by reframing the litigation on what is important -- a future for the children or starting to rebuild. When a client is refocused, it becomes easier to put a value on resolving the case with urgency outside of court. In determining value, I find it wise to counsel a client to take into consideration any support and/or costs that are being paid, the likely asset and debt split at trial and/or any attorney's fees and/or litigation costs. Many times, when these values can be established, they can be juxtaposed against what your client needs to rebuild their life and an offer of settlement can be crafted and extended accordingly.

What inspired you to become a Certified Family Law Specialist?

I started my legal career as a Civil Litigator. I worked closely with senior attorneys both inside and outside of the courtroom to master discovery, evidence and litigation techniques. In branching out on my own, I wanted to establish a practice in an area of law where I could impact people and assist them in their most difficult moments to take them through on to the next stage of their life.

I was inspired to become a Certified Family Law Specialist after years of practicing as a Family Law Attorney when I realized that there was a deeper level at which I could master my practice. Certifying as a specialist required me to demonstrate proficiency not only in family law, but in other areas of law that logically connect to divorce and family matters.

I opened my practice during a recession period -- a time that was difficult on families. I saw a lot of anger in the divorce process and a lot of families losing everything. Homes were being lost to foreclosure and savings accounts were being lost to attorneys. It was during that time that I really dug deep to come up with solutions. I turned to my certification in Alternative Dispute Resolution to brush off my mediation skills and develop a mediation program that would allow people to mediate their way through divorce thereby capping their fees and preserving their assets for splitting and equitable division.

I was also encountering many litigants who had been through multiple attorneys and were exhausted both emotionally and financially by the process. They just wanted to be done. This forced me to determine and guide clients through strategies that were guided by end-goal principles. Resources were so shallow that getting through the divorce was no longer the end-goal but speeding up the process and tightening the purse strings became priority. To that end, I found myself striving to educate myself in every aspect of Family Law and gain experiences that would be helpful in flushing out strategies designed at de-escalating conflict and/or getting through litigation in a manner that would allow people to still have life after the litigation.

What's the most important thing people with assets should consider when evaluating an Attorney?

Comfort is the first and foremost concern when working with an attorney. Potential clients should vet multiple attorneys and choose the attorney with whom they would feel most comfortable. Your legal advocate is someone in whom you will need to confide are share all facts -- good and bad. To that end, it is important that you feel comfortable intimately working with this person.

In addition to comfort, it is important to choose an advocate who is knowledgeable in family law but also comfortable with the processes that will move you forward in the process. For example, if you are not knowledgeable about the finances and/or assets of the marriage, then it may be important to work with someone who is strong in discovery and pulling facts out of the other side. If the goal is to litigate, then it is important to have an advocate who is strong in evidence and procedure. If the goal is out of court resolution, it will be important to pick an attorney who, while confident, can move forward without ego and can de-escalate the conflict while advocating for your position.

Many advocates believe that clients find attorneys who mirror their personalities. While evaluating an attorney, it may be worth evaluating why you like the attorney and ensuring that those reasons serve your best interests.

What are your final thoughts for people wanting to rebuild their lives after divorce?

It is common to feel overwhelmed during divorce. There is no question that the process will feel unfair. You may even fight the impulse not to disclose certain assets and/or finances because arguably they cannot take what they cannot find. Although common and normal reactions, none of this contributes to a successful divorce.

The most successful divorces are experienced by people who are able to (1) work with experienced and knowledgeable counsel; (2) develop a strategy; (3) execute on that strategy and (4) maintain perspective. Although the retention of counsel may seem expensive and complicated, the ability to get through the dissolution process in a strategic and goal-oriented manner may depend on the ability to rely on counsel. However, in order to be effective, counsel will need as much information as possible. This means that in order to allow your counsel to be as effective as possible, you should provide as much information as possible. Although time consuming, the information gathering process, is integral to streamlining any dissolution strategy. To the extent that you are served with documents and/or discovery, you should work diligently to ensure that your advocate has every piece of information necessary to move you forward in a manner that meets all deadlines are met. Putting in the time and effort today, preserves for your future tomorrow.

If someone feels they want to retain their resources, so they can rebuild their lives after divorce, how can they connect with you?

If you would like to start strategizing how you can best retain your assets through your divorce, give me a call at (877) 479-7970. Anyone on staff should be able to walk you through the brief intake process whereby you are asked some background information regarding your situation. You will then be put on calendar for a complimentary confidential no-obligation consultation during which we will be able to discuss your matter and arm you with enough information to make knowledgeable decisions to move you forward.

KATHLEEN RUANE LEEDY

Kathleen Ruane Leedy Mediation
Training/Consulting Services

Email: kathleen@kruaneleedy.com

Website: http://kruaneleedy.com

LinkedIn: Kathleen Ruane Leedy

Facebook: Kathleen Ruane Leedy

Call: (508)379-3111

My true belief and experience is that Mediation can unlock the deadlocks allowing people to have issue solving conversations, craft mutually beneficial agreements resulting in a rebuilding and repurposing of life! It is my mantra and the basis of how I teach others. I call it mediating with heart, another dimension added to the process, as many times mediators are mediating the emotional moments not the issues! Mediation is a pragmatic process that is dealing with human beings, so all dynamics need to be respected both the issues and the emotional intangibles!

A high school Health teacher for 21 years to a highly trained, experienced bi-coastal Mediator/Trainer/Consultant specializing in divorce, court issues, and high conflict-mediations is an honor, a privilege and a journey that all started with a serious injury that rendered me at a diminished capacity for 3 1/2 years. Now always having a heartbeat for people to learn and grow through and despite their life curveballs is my passion. The Mediation Table has room for all of it, and with easy, medium, and sometimes intense labor all can be resolved.

I enjoy working in Central Massachusetts, Greater Boston, and Tacoma/Seattle areas, with my private practice office in Gloucester, Massachusetts. Being on the list of the AGO in Massachusetts as one of their Open Meetings mediators is exciting and I recently completed the Facilitator Training presented by the consulting firm 'Community At Work' located in San Francisco, California.

I mediate divorces with restraining orders in place, mentor new mediators, train mediators, volunteer at Harvard to assist with their mediation role plays, speak at the college level in Washington state, and coach MIT graduate students in Cambridge, Massachusetts enrolled in the Negotiation and Conflict Management program.

I enjoy being the Court and Training Coordinator in a non-profit, and volunteering in a Probate court for a Mediation company in Boston, Massachusetts. The above mentioned variety is enjoyable, challenging, and gives me the ability to hone my skills, have the success of a 95% agreement rate, teach well, and be an enthusiastic lifelong learner.

Lastly, and mostly importantly to my beautiful, amazing daughters Jillian and Carley who in 1999, in 8th and 5th grades respectively, when our lives fell apart, stood by their broken Mother, through thick and thin, sickness and health to be at this place now altogether as a team! All my love!

WALKING WITH A MEDIATOR
THROUGH THE TRIP AND FALL WORLD
OF DIVORCE.
By Kathleen Ruane Leedy

Tell us about Kathleen Ruane Leedy Mediation Services, the people you help?

I help people seeking a cost effective divorce to come to harmonious agreements, so they can feel confident about moving forward toward a more productive and successful life.

All the people I work with have found themselves either by design or by happenstance approaching or at the crevice of a divorce. It's the word that means a split, subtraction not addition a severing, that which was one now will become two. Their lives now have to be divided before it can be grown again. It is loss before gain. It is such a loss that it creates a tailspin or vortex of swirling energies and thoughts and abilities.

An impending divorce impacts a person on all levels with varying degrees of hot and cold, fight and flight, sink or swim mentality. The shock to all their personal systems makes it hard for them to hit their personal go button in life. Go where, go how, and to where are now the issues! Add to the mix concerns for their children and it's quite a mess.

It doesn't matter which side of the abyss the person is on.... the future is now unknown. The situations they find themselves in are numerous of course and the big problem is all those situations can change like the weather the next day, week, or month so now all has to be renegotiated by their already stressed out mind and emotions.

The formula for success here is to have a safe process with a strongly buckled seat belt to hang on for the ride, that achieves agreements. A healthy Mediation is that safe process and a skilled Mediator is that guide and the human safety belt. A successful mediation process will have healthy outcomes. A skilled mediator directs a good mediation which navigates the wild ride. The results of being firmly held in place through the process by a skilled professional is peace, and acceptance, and confidence, that moving forward will be successful because all the moving pieces have been examined and resolved.

What are the advantages of seeking a cost effective divorce?

Well the advantages of seeking a cost effective divorce is that monies spent in the process are gone, and not for future use, so spending as little as possible is wise. Divorce is breaking a financial union which normally conserves monies. In a marriage people usually share items like the house, the cars, the bills etc. The more funds a divorcing couple have for their new single life is to their advantage.

Harmonious agreements come from harmony being part of the process which lessens emotional draining, increasing the ability to think well. This is the Mediator's responsibility as they conduct the process. Agreements become harmonious because of a person actually truly agrees with their own best thinking, (harmony from within), and feels confident to vocalize it at the Mediation Table.

Agreeing is sacred ground where each person is valuing what is important to them and then considering what to keep, what to let go of, and when to compromise. The outcome percentages of each issue resolved are not often 50/50 but the final outcome, which is the written mediated agreement called an MOU often times is. The walkaway factor of satisfaction is truly desirable.

What do you feel are some of the biggest myths about divorce mediation?

Oh yes there are some big myths out there in regard to divorce mediation! One of the myths is that I can't stand him or her therefore I can't and won't mediate with them! The answer is yes you can, because you start out talking to the Mediator and can continue to talk only to the mediator until your comfort zone extends to the other person. The process of joint and private sessions in mediation allow the comfort zone of each person to grow and gains the confidence to speak with each other in a productive manner without devastating consequences or drama or being bullied.

Another myth is that the courtroom is the best place to duke it out to finalize a divorce! The answer is often no because court is where you or your lawyer present your arguments/wants and the Judge decides the outcome for your life. Mediation is the process where the people at the table decide about their lives. We all bring our 'humanness' to every process including Judges. In court I was with a Judge that become impatient with the arguing dynamics and insist I mediate the remaining issues. In fairness often times the arguing is important to the people but not to the law. Judges are people too and get overwhelmed/annoyed with the infighting. Mediators are trained neutrals and know how to look past the intensity to the root of the issues which we call interests. Judges work at a feverish pace to apply justice in courtrooms that are scheduled out for months and deserve not to be burdened with issues trivial to the law.

Another myth is that all Mediators are the same and the answer is NO! We are not even all trained exactly the same. The most important thing about a Mediation is the mediator and the skills they bring to the table. How they think is very important as well. The best mediators are equally good at being pragmatic but also recognizing and being trained in handling the hot emotional triggers. I train Mediators and know the emotional realm is where most are weak.

Lastly people think they cannot bring their attorney to mediation and the answer is yes. It is very good to have attorneys present in mediation as they are experts on legal information which the mediation may require. Most lawyers are very respectful of the process and allow the mediator to conduct it.

What are some common misconceptions around the Alternative Dispute Resolution (ADR) industry?

There are some common misconceptions about the industry of ADR because we mostly get through life without it! It's not a familiar process like my process of going to the gas station twice a week as I travel from Worcester to Gloucester in Massachusetts, where I am familiar with the credit card slot, the grade gas my car needs and the best stations along the way. ADR is for a legal conflict, but pause and hold, because the conflict can be worked on and resolved before court! Some companies have a form or more than one form of ADR available to resolve legal disputes instead of court!

Another common misconception is that all forms of ADR are the same and that is not so. ADR is always about settling matters with a third party present but never the same process. Here is a list of what is available in the industry. ADR consists of negotiation, arbitration, both binding and non-binding, conciliation, collaborative law, conflict resolution, dispute resolution, and Lawyer-supported Mediation They are slightly or largely different from each other. Mediation is very special as it has two layers of confidentiality, mediators are not mandated reporters, our notes are destroyed after the mediation ends, we can settle below or above the law with valid explanation, and with rare exceptions even a Judge cannot make us testify in court!

What are some of the most common fears about mediation?

Most people have not participated in a mediation so having fears or being anxious about an unfamiliar process is common and understandable! Usually there are questions about the process and not particular fears, but common concerns are: how long does a mediation usually last, will the other person really listen to me, is it a legal process, will it work because we have already been fighting over and over about the same issues with no progress, what is a mediated agreement, can mediation really make a difference, will I get a chance to be really heard, I can't stand them so why would I want to be in the same room with them! Many people are the dominant or a quieter partner and the concerns swing both ways.... will he/she ever stop talking or finally start talking! Sometimes people are truly afraid to be in the same room with each other and there are some ways to handle that as well!

How can people seeking a cost effective divorce mediation solve those fears?

Most concerning issues and questions get addressed during the free phone call intake process before people agree to mediate. There are always questions about the process and we just take our time together and I answer all the questions and address the fears/concerns. It is important to let people know that many people feel the same way, so they are not unusual. Right out of the gate mediation is cheaper than litigation so there is a cost savings which helps people get past their concerns.

Mediation is a process, but the process can be tailored to meet any unique concerns. There are many ways to tweak the process to help people feel less fearful.

For example:

1. Mediation can be done in a shuttle style in two different rooms where people never see each other and communicate through the mediator and by addressing and approving issues in writing.

2. Mediation can actually begin by addressing the fears and concerns or the questions. When the matters are settled then we can move forward into the issues.

3. Mediation can begin with private sessions where parties can vent and let off steam and share truly private information or concerns they don't want to say in front of the other person.

4. Mediation is truly a voluntary process, so people can walk away and not continue or at least take a break and come back.

5. Mediation sessions can be different lengths of time usually ranging from two to four hours.

6. Mediators use a skill called reiteration where a person's words are summarized in an exact manner so what was just spoken is crystal clear with no misunderstanding. All

these tactics and skills relax the environment, so people can feel comfortable and validated which enables issues to get resolved!

What other perceived obstacles do you see that might be preventing people from seeking the help of a Divorce Mediator?

A big obstacle is that most people think that there is too much to be undone and to talk about. Think of a long marriage and all the decisions made and all the things purchased, and all the history people have with family, and time invested etc. It's like an attic filled with stuff and now they have to go clean out the attic and deal with all the stuff! Just thinking about it is exhausting never mind dealing with each item and deciding what to do with it. That is the biggest perceived obstacle.... the dread factor of having to face all the stuff of the past, how to divide it all up, and then think of a new life on top of a life that is in ashes!

It is a crazy swirling world and it seems easier to give it to an attorney and be done with it! The problem is that the attorney has not lived their lives, and is trained to and sworn to uphold the law which is not always paying attention to unique individual needs, wants, and desires. Also there is not much healing in that decision, lawyers charge more, litigation forces people to take sides and fight for what they want instead of start to heal. Then there is the unfortunate as some attorneys choose to escalate the battle to get more money for themselves. Divorces can cost thousands of dollars in litigation mainly due to the discovery process which is very important but not a procedure followed in Mediation.

Another perceived obstacle is that mediators don't have the expertise on financial, insurance, retirement issues etc. so how can the mediation document be concise and accurate. This is a fair question that can be easily overcome by the mediator have outside sources to assist as a financial neutral in the expertise components of the mediation. Just ask the mediator if they have a list of these types of resources and then confidence in that part of the process can be achieved.

What are some of the mistakes you see people in long-term or older age marriages make when seeking a divorce?

People in long-term marriages either make the mistake or thinking they should have too much or not enough. It's a different dynamic because they have been together so long, partners in life, often raising each other starting in their late teens or early twenties. There is usually the 'more' factor! More guilt, exhaustion, apathy, regrets, anger, sadness etc. just because of the longevity of time and experience together. The more factor interferes with their legal decisions the state needs for a proper divorce. For instance, someone may have more guilt and want to give the other person the house free and clear and get no compensation for it. In mediation this can happen, but we have to make double sure this is really what they want and there won't be any regrets down the road. Then we have to provide the supporting language to explain the unique decision.

Other mistakes that can happen in in long-term marriage and/or older age divorces are mistakes with taxes, insurances, alimony, and retirement where one person gets too much and the other person not enough. The law looks at a long-term marriage with a lot of respect and sees most issues at 50/50 value, so mediation needs to bring that to their attention. The law also is sensitive to the financial fragility of an older age divorce with the importance of both people living a quality life as possible into their shorter rather than longer possible futures.

How can these mistakes be avoided?

The unique mistakes made in a long-term or older age marriage can be avoided by asking quality open ended questions. These questions will encourage them to take a look forward, envisioning their new life, and talking in joint and private sessions at length to help them see the value they are gaining or letting go of. What will your life look like to you? is an example of an open ended question that can promote a productive discussion.

These mistakes can also be avoided by creating a timeline for reference and writing it out on a piece of paper, a concrete way of discussing an idea. Writing out a timeline for a 2 year, 5 year, a 10 year plan because long-term marriages and older age divorces are usually ending in the back one half or one third of life and seeing it laid out on paper increases the reality of thinking that they are capable of living out the plan.

Share an example of how you have helped someone overcome obstacles and succeed in coming to a harmonious agreement?

In healthy well run divorce mediation, people are always overcoming their obstacles, but some cases are more dramatic than others. Of the several I have in my mind one stands out because the one person was just released from Federal prison for assault and injury to three other people and now wanted parenting time with their five year old child. Today both parents were in Probate court appearing before a Judge.

In most states, if not every state, Parenting Time can be modified and changed in court to reflect new circumstances in each parent's life. In this case both parents agreed that the parent just out of prison with a restraining order in place was a good and loving parent! The hurdles and obstacles that needed overcoming was for the one parent that had been abused by the other to give a second chance and the other parent had to put aside the jail culture of power, having their every move controlled therefore not needing to think, feel or make decisions and always blaming others.

In the extra layer of confidentiality in the private session I kept asking the restraining order parent what they wanted, and they kept blaming everyone else about everything blah, blah,

blah! Finally I said "enough", and I have heard you now five times blame all involved for everything! As your mediator I want to know what do you want! The parent looked at me, eyes became huge and tearing up and got very quiet even hanging their head. He said without looking at me 'nobody ever asks me what I want'. I said, 'well I am, what do you want'? I waited for what seemed like eternity and finally looking up at me straight in the eye there was a whisper that gained energy and he blurted out 'I want her to trust me again"! I smiled and bounded out of my seat and said 'I can work with that' I will be back.

In 10 minutes I was back after sitting with the other parent shaking like a leaf being so willing to give that second chance but afraid of the past and finally saying yes! The courage in action that day was unforgettable to me forever! Each parent had their demons to face and they both squared up and chose 'grace'…. giving favor to where it wasn't deserved. Wow!

This is the potential healing power of mediation and why me and others are dedicated to it!

What led you to becoming a Divorce Mediator, what's your backstory?

My story of becoming a Mediator is really quite a random event seemingly. It started by socializing and listening intently one Wednesday night in Atlanta, in 2009, while pilots were discussing the upcoming than private merger in-the-making deal between AirTran and Southwest. They were discussing options and I kept coming up with more adding them to the pot. Eventually one of the Captain's turned to me and said Kathleen you should become a Mediator! My immediate response was…. what is a mediator? The next day I called my daughters and sister and told them about the comment and everyone agreed I would be great, but no one knew what a Mediator was!

I think the word impacted us and it sounded like what I had done all day as a high school Health teacher, mediating between students, parents, and administration! Two weeks later I signed up for a 40 hr. Basic Mediation class in Atlanta and found myself mistakenly partnering with a Superior Court Judge who asked me if I had done my homework last night and the journey began!

What are your final thoughts for anyone who wants to come to harmonious agreements during the mediation process?

Divorce can rarely be done well without a process run by a 3rd party. The power of having communications clarified by the mediator to achieve harmony has tremendous value during the divorce process but also pays dividends after the divorce is complete. Many couples like to proclaim how amicable their divorce was giving themselves pats on the back about their personal goodness etc. as they should!

Harmonious agreements helps prevent the negativity factor from taking on a life of its own in people's comments therefore dominating the divorce mediation process. The process of harmony usually is a win for both people allowing them still not to like each other if so desired but acknowledging that good decisions can be made anyway. In addition the communication skills that are built in mediation, keeping it harmonious, carry forward in life interactions beyond the Mediation Table.

What's the most important thing people seeking a cost effective divorce should consider when evaluating a Divorce Mediator?

There are many important factors in seeking first a cost effective divorce mediation and then secondly evaluating mediators in regard to their divorce mediation process. From the onset Mediation is cheaper per hour than litigation. I recommend asking the following questions.

1. Always ask the mediator their agreement rate percentage and how many cases they have completed. A mediator's experience and success at the mediation table is very important as the more mediations they conduct the better they can become, but the percentage of their agreement reveals their parties' successes. Their fluidly at running a good effective process keeps the cost down due to fewer sessions.

2. Secondly, personality is important as that sets the tone of the mediations because the mediator brings their personality to the table as well as running the process. So do you feel comfortable with them is a great answer to have. Do you feel understood by them is important. Did they cut you off in the phone conversation? That is a red flag because Mediators are trained to listen. If they cut you off on a simple phone call it will certainly happen in a difficult moment in mediation and your voice won't be fully heard.

3. How long is each session is important to ask. My mediations are mostly three hours to lessen the back and forth of multiple visits impacting personal/work schedules but also that 3rd hour together is where most of the agreements happen and we don't have to begin with a fresh discussion on another day. We have endings and the next session can start with beginnings.

4. Did they talk about the money a lot? Most good mediators have money on their mind last not first because mediation is ultimately a healing business where people are more important than the funds.

5. Does the mediator have a panel of experts for the parties to access? Financial experts are especially important that can come to the table as a 'neutral expert' to explain insurances, 401K, taxes, etc., as well to answer questions, and then also run potential options by each person to help with good decision making.

6. What are the office hours? This is an important question to ask because after work hours doesn't impacts their income both ways. One way paying the mediator and secondly missing work to mediate therefore lowering the paycheck.

If someone wants to come to harmonious agreements, so they can feel confident about moving forward toward a more productive and successful life, how can they connect with you?

In moving forward toward my divorce mediation process I like to connect with people by telephone, so either calling me at (508)379-3111, or emailing me at kathleen@kruaneleedy.com with times to call back is best. The first phone call is free no matter the length. This phone process allows us to meet each other by voice and allows people to decide whether they feel comfortable, and build confidence about the process and myself. We will chat about the particulars, conduct an intake process, and then I email all necessary documents to move forward.

This is the time to ask the many questions that may be in a person's mind. The next step would be reaching out to the spouse/partner asking them to contact me as well if there is a mutual interest to mediate. If not, I can be that person's mediator/facilitator during the divorce process and work with their attorney, or the process forward if the other person represents themselves pro se in court.

CARLTON R. MARCYAN

Attorney CPA Schiller DuCanto & Fleck LLP

Email: CRMJDCPA@yahoo.com

Website: http://sdflaw.com

LinkedIn: http//linkedin.com/in/carltonmarcyan

Call: (847)604-6005

With more than 30 years of law practice, Marcyan has had much opportunity to employ his skills as a certified public accountant, CERTIFIED FINANCIAL PLANNER™ and litigator to successfully represent clients. No stranger to the courtroom, Marcyan is recognized by his peers and judiciary as top divorce litigator. Martindale Hubbell awarded him its highest rating, AV; Super Lawyers as the top 100 of all lawyers in Illinois and Best Lawyers, Divorce Lawyer of the Year and Collaborative Divorce Lawyer of the Year many times.

Marcyan's practice includes not only litigation but alternative resolution methods such as mediation and Collaborative Law when leading his clients through divorce. He is known for his professional style and ability to reduce conflict and anxiety and promote resolution in a more harmonious way. However, when needed, he is a force to be reckoned with in the courtroom.

He is past Chair of his firm, Schiller DuCanto & Fleck LLP, leading it for more than seven years. It is the largest firm in the country exclusively practicing matrimonial law and widely recognized as one of the nation's top divorce firms.

WHY YOU DESERVE THE
BEST POSSIBLE REPRESENTATION
By Carlton R. Marcyan

Tell us about Schiller DuCanto & Fleck LLP, the clients you help and the types of situations they find themselves in when in need of professional guidance?

I guide, in a dignified manner, mature, wealthy people through the changes caused by divorce, providing them peace of mind and a stable financial future.

Divorce, at any age, is a difficult process that takes a financial and emotional toll. Having practiced in this area of the law for more than 30 years I have been "in the trenches" with my clients helping them go through one of the most difficult times in their lives. During the recent past years there has been a swelling in the divorce rate of those with long marriages; the so-called "Graying Divorce". There are unique problems associated with these divorces such as health of the spouses, large extended families and numerous and valuable assets of complexity that need careful consideration when getting divided as part of the divorce.

My firm, Schiller DuCanto & Fleck, LLP has been in existence for over 35 years, and I have been there almost since its beginning. Our speciality is financially complex cases requiring unique expertise and experience to properly handle them. Through a combination of expertise, experience and empathy I and my firm are particularly qualified to properly guide a mature client through the labyrinth of the divorce process to a successful result.

Quite often estates contain significant retirement assets, partnership interests, annuities, businesses and complex trusts. A CPA and CERTIFIED FINANCIAL PLANNER™ certificates coupled with a MBA degree and law license gives me the background and savvy to understand these complexities and be well-able to determine their value and divide them while taking advantage of possible tax benefits.

What are the advantages of getting divorced in a dignified manner?

Emotions run high during a divorce. Psychologists have established that the logical part of our thinking is disabled when you become angered, fearful or under stress. At a time when you need your logical abilities the most, you are the greatest disadvantage because your raw emotions have taken hold and your "fight or flight" response has engaged. This is why it is important to have a lawyer who can assist you; however, you do not want an attorney that is magnifying your emotions as you are then driven into more illogic. What you need is counsel that helps you tone down those emotions bringing your mind back to logic and thoughtfulness.

In almost all instances more can be achieved through a process where respect for each other is maintained. In the circumstances the parties are much more likely appreciative of the financial and psychological value of thoughtfully analyzing the situation and looking for choices that do not destroy the estate. Generally, treating others in a dignified way invites a similar response. Admittedly, some people are less capable of allowing themselves to engage in a mutually beneficial process and want to "hammer" the other side for whatever reason. Sophisticated divorce counsel has seen this all before and can change the approach to counter this kind of behavior either by becoming more aggressive or taking an approach that can disarm the other side by revealing to the court the "antics" of the other side.

What do you feel are some of the biggest myths about the divorce process?

The "Top 10" greatest myths about divorce are:

My divorce will cost me a fortune: In fact many times the divorce process can go quite efficiently. Also, there are alternatives to traditional litigation that many times result in a less cost to both parties.

I can represent myself and do not need a lawyer: Very few people who are not trained in the law can adequately deal with the lawyer on the other side and the judge. Remember, the adage "He who represents himself has a fool for a client" is largely accurate.

You must go to court to "fight it out": There are other pathways to resolution that do not include court. Mediation with a trained mediator and Collaborative Law are two widely accepted methods that avoid court and greatly lessen the cost.

A divorce will take a long time: Especially when using the Mediation or Collaborative approach a case does not have to take years to complete. These alternative methods allow for more concentrated and quality time then going to court every 60 days to report to the court.

Me and my spouse will become bitter enemies: Not necessarily true; there are instances where both spouses understand that "life moves on" and people can grow apart. Generally, using the Mediation or the Collaborative approach is conducive to allowing the parties to maintain cordial relationship and, if there are children, promotes cooperation to the benefit of the family

I need a lawyer that is a "Junkyard Dog": Great lawyers are able to control their own emotions and act in a manner most appropriate for the facts and circumstances of the case. As the saying goes "You can draw more bees to honey than with vinegar." Even in instances where the lawyer needs to get tough the better approach is to have an "iron fist in a velvet glove". Judges appreciate the subtlety of controlled strength rather than outright antagonism.

I don't need a lawyer that is "good at numbers", just a fighter: Time and time again lawyers who just are antagonistic and want to "beat up" the other side lose sight of the goals of the case and just run up fees without result. Their antics turn out to be a showcase for their client who thinks they are winning but, in fact, losing.

I don't need a lawyer that specializes in divorce: Like it or not we are in the age of specialization. The state and federal laws are too complex and case law has too many nuances for general practice lawyers to appreciate. Also, lawyer who specialize are in the same of the same judges who come to know them and develop trust in the best lawyers.

I am too old to get divorced: As people near retirement age and spend more time together they find that their interests are not the same and what they had in common in the 20's is no longer in their 60's. Rather than trying to maintain a "demilitarized zone" in their home, it may be healthier to understand that they should both move on separately.

Everybody loses in divorce but the lawyers: Good counsel can divide assets to great tax advantage to both sides creating a "Win-Win". For example, dividing retirement funds can be done through specialized court orders that allow tax-free transfers and sometimes can avoid early withdrawal penalties.

What are some common misconceptions around the legal industry?

Lawyers are in it for themselves: Many times you hear people say that lawyers are in it for themselves and they do not have the client's best interest at heart. While there are always a few "bad apples" my experience is that the vast majority of lawyers want to help their clients through hard times and do their very best for them. Most lawyers are so because they are problem solvers and want to help others. Sure, there is also a profit motive, but economic reward is best when working hard and smartly for a client and achieving a great result.

Judges could care less: In all my 30+ years of experience I have only encountered one or two judges who really did not care, and they were either at the end of their career or were going through psychological issues. Judges do care and are dedicated to moving their caseloads and getting cases to conclusion; however, many times they are overwhelmed by the volume of their calls. The best lawyers make cases interesting for the court and demonstrate its unique characteristics and "humanize" their client to the judge. Judges are human too! They relate and respond to the human condition.

The case will go on forever: The legal process can be tedious and time consuming. This is largely do to the rules of the court system allowing each side adequate time to file papers, respond to the other side's papers, take depositions and prepare for trial. The best lawyers know how to streamline the process and move a case along. A judge who is backed up with his or her "call" will have cases that take longer. This is why alternative methods such as Mediation and Collaborative Law are good alternatives. Schedules and timetables can be greatly accelerated with these other methods.

What do mature, wealthy people fear about getting divorced?

The divorce process is widely feared as highly conflictual and unsavory. This is especially so among the more mature and wealthy clients who have grave concern that not only is there great cost but that their lives will become an "open book" invading their privacy and revealing their finances, child custody issues and dalliances.

Additionally, anxiety about the future and ability to maintain a pre-divorce lifestyle frequently is an impediment to settlement. Generally the more financially unsophisticated spouse has a very difficult time accepting the split and delays conclusion mainly because of not wanting to let go.

It is especially necessary to have legal representation that can "think out of the box" and suggest a creative process that preserves privacy by avoiding publication in the court record of a litigants' intimate, financial, family and amorous details. Both mediation and Collaborative process provide such safeguards and preservation of privacy. They are also methods that reduce conflict and are forums in which conflict can be better managed or eliminated altogether. Finally, one of the most important factors in a divorce is lifestyle. Having a lawyer that understands how to quantify it and demonstrate to and convince the mediator and court of the amount of cash flow and funds needed to support this lifestyle is critical.

What should people do to get past those fears?

Many times the best way to conquer fear is to directly confront it. Avoiding the school yard bully just invites him back time and time again. Dealing with the problem is the best way to stop resolve it. Similarly, in a divorce case, you need your "bodyguard", i.e. lawyer, to help you deal with the the harassment and attacks of the other side and his lawyer. An able advocate will have the training, experience and savvy to "deflect the blows" and have turn them around in your favor. A great lawyer is not only well versed in the law but your confidant and gladiator.

Consider an alternative method like Mediation or Collaborative Law. These allow for a wider range of options as to how meetings are conducted and issues are addressed. The traditional litigation process can be monolithic and uninviting to other than an adversarial process.

Hire a divorce coach to help you cope with the emotional issues and anxiety that accompany the process. Many times the lawyers do not have time to do a "deep dive" with the client in his or her emotional conflicts. Having a trained divorce coach provides that outlet and better develops coping mechanisms.

What other perceived obstacles do you see that might be preventing mature, wealthy people from seeking the help of an Attorney CPA?

The single biggest reason for not taking action is inertia. It is defined as "... continuing an existing state of rest or motion in a straight line. It can only be changed by an external force." The same thing occurs with people; unless an external force moves them otherwise, people will generally continue the same course and not change. Especially for those mature and wealthy clients, they need to understand that divorce is a unique situation that requires new outlook and new approach to problem solving. They need to seek the best representation possible and a lawyer who is not only well versed in the law but has acquired other training that brings invaluable understanding to the process. That is why a lawyer who is recognized as an exceptional litigator who also has a CPA background is worth his weight in gold.

When it comes to divorcing in a dignified manner, what are some of the common mistakes you see mature, wealthy people make?

The single biggest mistake that mature, wealthy people make when divorcing is their reluctance to sit down with the other side, with counsel present, to discuss what the own, owe, have income-wise, their financial needs for the future, goals and fears. This kind of communication dispels misconceptions and can bring about a joint solution while avoiding misconceptions and antagonism. Good lawyers can draw this information from the clients and demonstrate that dialogue can be pathway to speedy resolution.

Other mistakes are:

- Failing to recognize the value of assets such as intellectual property that the other spouse may have created. Examples are software, literary work, patent, trademark or the like. The value of a business owned by a spouse is also frequently neglected considering that there may be the intangible value of goodwill to be considered. There are attorneys who specialize in intellectual property that can assist.

- Retirement benefits to which a spouse may be entitled but are not easily noticed or easily camouflaged. Unfunded pension or deferred compensation agreements are some examples of this.

- Failure to review the past few years of accounts and investment to see if funds have suddenly "evaporated". A spouse may have been spending on another person by withdrawing money from various accounts. Such unwarranted use of family assets is called "dissipation" and the divorce law in most states provides for a remedy.

- Requiring the other spouse to continue to maintain life insurance on his life for the benefit of the other.

- Failure to recognize the intrinsic value of insurance policies. Especially for the more mature person, all those years of paying in premiums may have resulted in the build-up of tremendous value that may go unnoticed.

How can these mistakes be avoided?

Getting the best and most experienced professional who is talented not only in the law but accounting, taxation, negotiation, business and the respect of the court is the pathway to successfully getting through a divorce for litigants with wealth and is especially true for those older, more mature clients who have substantial wealth and do not have time to go through multiple attorneys in their divorce. You need to get it "right the first time".

It may be necessary to retain, along with counsel, a forensic accountant to determine the appropriate value of assets. These accountants are highly trained and bring valuable insight. An experienced lawyer will have a number of forensic experts he or she has worked with in the past and found reliable.

Additionally, the forensic expert may have the acumen to decipher the existence and real value of unfunded retirement interests. Bringing in a employee benefit expert can help out with this determination. Similarly, bringing aboard the "team" an insurance planner can decode the intricacies of insurance coverage and policies. These are often difficult to determine unless you have been in the industry and know the jargon.

Please share an example that really sums up how you've been able to help mature, wealthy people to overcome obstacles and succeed in gaining peace of mind and a stable financial future.

Recently I represented a gentleman who had been married more than 30 years who just wanted to live his own life on his boat out East. He had worked hard over the years supporting his wife and child as a consultant. Through his efforts and his wife's industriousness they amassed quite a sum of more than 8 million dollars and a beautiful home in the Northshore area of Chicago. When he informed his wife that he wanted to get a divorce and live out East on his boat she was understandably devastated.

After contacting her lawyer we were able to demonstrate to her and her attorney that the 4 million dollars she would receive in combination of investments and retirement account would leave her with more than substantial assets for the rest of her life. We analyzed her spending patterns and developed a quantification of her recent lifestyle. With the assets she was to receive we also, with the aid of a financial expert, calculated the cash flow that these would generate and be more than sufficient to cover her necessary as well as discretionary expenses for the rest of her life and still have money left over!

What inspired you to become an Attorney CPA, what's your backstory?

When first attending college my career path, as chose by my parents, was to become a doctor. After a few semesters I realized that I really had no interest in the natural sciences and began exploring other majors. A great friend of mine, now a prominent real estate attorney in Chicago, Michael Brennock, suggested I try the field of accounting and consider the law as well. This was his career pathway and thought it would be good for me as well.

Having watched the Perry Mason TV show as a youngster and finding out that, once I changed majors, I excelled in accounting, directed my attention to law school. While in law school I worked as a researcher for the IRS and the years prior to law school and after worked for a major accounting firm now known as PricewaterhouseCoopers where I worked as an auditor and tax specialist. Then, very fortunately, I through the aid of another good friend and now retired judge, Gregory O'Brien, got an associate position at my firm where I have been since 1983. Schiller DuCanto & Fleck, LLP is the preeminent and largest divorce firm in the country with almost 50 lawyers. My background in accounting, taxation and litigation turned out to be exceptional training to become a divorce lawyer handling complicated financial cases.

So, when all was said and done, my inspiration was Perry Mason and two very good friends that I have known for almost 50 years. One finds out that in life we rarely do things alone; it is our real friends that help us.

What's the most important thing people should consider when evaluating an Attorney CPA?

The most important factors to keep in mind when choosing a divorce lawyer are:

1. Do I have good chemistry with this person, i.e. can I work with him or her?

2. Docs the lawyer have the technical abilities to understand and use the laws of divorce, taxation and command over "the numbers" to fully represent my interests and get a great result?

3. Is the lawyer knowledgeable about the court system and known by the judges who hear these cases?

4. Does the lawyer have adequate support staff to help get the job done?

5. Is the lawyer honest, can I trust him or her?

6. Is this lawyer respected by his or her peers?

7. Does this lawyer always do cases the same way or "think out of the box" and be creative?

8. Is this lawyer accessible?

9. If my case has to "go to war", is he or she not only capable but willing to be my champion?

10. Is this lawyer capable of going to trial if need be?

What are your final thoughts for people considering divorce who want to have peace of mind and a stable financial future?

Find the best lawyer you can afford; use the checklists I provide above and put your trust in the lawyer. A divorce lawyer who has a CPA with experience and training in accounting, taxation and a great courtroom lawyer is the best combination.

If someone feels they want to get divorced in a dignified manner, so they can have peace of mind and a stable financial future, how can they connect with you?

In this day in age there are many ways to get in touch. The most direct is to call at (847) 604-6005. You can also email me at CMarcyan@sdflaw.com. Because of my unique background I am asked to represent clients all over the country, so even if your case is not in the Chicago area, I can still provide you valuable representation and the best possible result.

ABOUT THE AUTHOR

Mark Imperial is a Best Selling Author, Syndicated Business Columnist, Syndicated Radio Host, and internationally recognized Stage, Screen, and Radio Host of numerous business shows spotlighting leading experts, entrepreneurs, and business celebrities.

His passion is discovering noteworthy business owners, professionals, experts, and leaders who do great work, and sharing their stories and secrets to their success with the world on his syndicated radio program titled "Remarkable Radio".

Mark is also the media marketing strategist and voice for some of the world's most famous brands. You can hear his voice over the airwaves weekly on Chicago radio and worldwide on iHeart Radio.

Mark is a Karate black belt, teaches kickboxing, loves Thai food, House Music, and his favorite TV show is infomercials.

Learn more:

www.MarkImperial.com
www.ImperialAction.com
www.RemarkableRadioShow.com

www.ingramcontent.com/pod-product-compliance
Lightning Source LLC
Chambersburg PA
CBHW072154090426

42740CB00012B/2256